AND THE CAPSTONE

Lessons Learned about Life and Leadership

DAVID A. MILLER

Printed in the United States of America

For additional copies or information contact David A. Miller: david@davidmiller.pro

Design: Soundview Design

First Printing, 2022

ISBN: 978-1-7923-8595-7

To my mom and dad who not only taught me about the One who is the Cornerstone and Capstone, but also lived out His message of grace and truth

To my children who are teaching me much more than I ever taught them

To my friend, G. Randall Andrews whose heart is much bigger than his pocketbook

TABLE OF CONTENTS

FOREWORD

A hero to me is someone who dedicates their life to making a difference in the lives of others. David Miller is one of my heroes. He's both a dreamer and a doer, a truth seeker and a problem solver, and he's one of the most inspirational and principled leaders I have ever been around.

I first met David at Spirt Ranch, a leadership development and team building center that David founded. My brother, Kally, said that I should meet him and introduced us at the ranch in the Escondido Canyon just north of Lubbock, Texas. I remember our first encounter like it was yesterday. I was most impressed with his clarity of purpose and passion for people. Whether he was leading his company as CEO, our community as Mayor, or the nonprofit he started, David's success was undoubtedly a result of his calling, clear thinking, and commitment to serving others.

From that day forward, David and I have developed a very special friendship, and I have always admired his courage, character, and extraordinary God-given talents. I've never forgotten what he told me about sticking with these simple yet profound principles of leadership and I've been well-served to put them into practice in my life.

When he asked me to write the forward to The Four Cornerstones and the Capstone, I was honored and excited to have the opportunity. I believe the cornerstone principles David has captured on the following pages, if applied, will not only improve your life and leadership, but also help in leading your family, profession, and our nation to a stronger foundation and more positive outcomes.

David's approach to life and leadership resonates with me

for three main reasons. First, as I mentioned, he makes it simple. He has distilled the dozens, if not hundreds, of ideas on leadership into five consumable packages which he has entitled, "trust, understanding, freedom, unity, and joy." It's easy to get overwhelmed with so much sage leadership advice from so many sources. I find it almost impossible to digest it all in any meaningful way. But to meditate on the richness of these five principles and savor their impact has strengthened me in my roles as a husband, father, and Member of Congress.

Second, David is a great storyteller. His compelling antidotes and vignettes not only illustrate the fine points of the cornerstones, but they inspire! As David writes, the stories "breathe life" into our hearts and enhance our understanding. When I think of building a legacy, I think in terms of the stories I will leave behind. What stories will you create with your life? What will they say about you and your impact? David shows us how we can live a life of purpose and consequence if we build our lives on these foundational principles.

Finally, I love how David authentically weaves spiritual lessons throughout the book. In each chapter, there are examples of faith that can and will sustain us. Without forcing his beliefs on us, David humbly offers these timeless truths for all to consider. In the latter part of the book, he has given us even more stories along with Bible references and journal pages to use as we contemplate our own journey.

I highly recommend you read, reflect, and live out the nuggets of gold you'll find in the following pages, and, as you do, may God bless you in your journey.

– Jodey Arrington, United States Congressman 19th District of the State of Texas

INTRODUCTION

I'm 72 years old as I pen this introduction. The words that appear on the following pages have been in my head and heart for too many years and they need to "get out". That being said, I'm pretty certain that the world doesn't need another book on leadership. Collins, Brown, Covey, Lencioni, Blanchard, Drucker, Peters, Gladwell, Sinek, Maxwell, Biehl, Cloud, Townsend[1]. Haven't they and others pretty well said it all? So why would I impose my thoughts on you via a book of my own?

Well, partly because I need to write it...for me. To "dare greatly" as Teddy Roosevelt said[2]. And, partly because I do think there is *more* to be learned as both you and I examine our own leadership of others. You'll read more about *more* in the ensuing pages. And, finally because I need to write it to honor my personal mission statement which is stated for you below.

For the first three decades of my career I was a business executive almost always finding myself in the CEO's chair. For the last 15 years or so I've been what the experts call a leadership coach. I don't put myself in the category of being an expert and I don't hold any kind of professional certification, but the label of coach fits pretty well.

As a coach one of the most important challenges I give the leaders I coach is that of writing their own personal purpose, mission, vision, and values statements. It seems that very few of us ever have invested the time, thought, and energy into developing these directional imperatives. Instead, most folks either relentlessly pursue lofty goals or, on the other hand, just drift through life letting things happen as they may. I don't see anything wrong with either of those paths other than when people look back on their lives (much like a 72 year old guy might do), they wonder what have I done and why did I do it?

Throughout my career I had helped craft purpose, mission, vision, and values statements for the companies I worked for. And they were not just a catchy slogan that was put in a framed poster in the board room. They genuinely guided our decisions over the course of time.

But, then sometime in my mid-50's I began working on a personal mission statement for my life. I didn't even know where to begin, but fortunately I came across a book by Laurie Beth Jones[3] titled *The Path*. From the pages of that book I discovered a process by which I could develop my mission statement. With only minor changes during the past 15 years that statement remains the same. My mission is to *Seek, Live, Share Truth.*

Four words…three action verbs (seek, live, share)…one subject (Truth). Brevity. Laser focus. I want to always be seeking as a life-long learner because there's always *more* to know. I want to authentically live out the time tested principles that I've discovered. And if the things I've learned and lived really are valuable I want to share them with you. And what is Truth? In my coaching sessions I say that truth is "stuff that works". For me personally, Jesus Christ is the Truth.[4] You'll read a story later how knowing my mission rather than just responding or reacting to external circumstances completely changed my life and career path.

I have learned a mission statement alone is not enough. I mentioned above the challenge of developing (and living out) purpose, vision, and values statements, too. What's the difference? Here is a brief explanation but in the appendix in the back of the book you will find more detailed information and worksheets that will help you develop your personal statements.

Your purpose statement answers the "why" question. Why are you here...on earth? Why do you do what you do? This always requires a great deal of soul searching and inevitably leads to more "why" questions.

Your mission statement answers the "what" question. What do you do? Not your job description as a banker, homemaker, ballplayer or doctor. Regardless of your employer or title, what do you do?

Your vision statement paints a picture of what it looks like when you are being successful in pursuing your purpose and accomplishing your mission. It's the emotion of "yes!" when you know it feels right.

Your values statement lists what character traits are most important to you. They are what you hold dear and want to be known for by sticking with them. They are standards you strive to live up to.

So since one part of my mission is to share "stuff that works" with you, I've made a compilation of such stuff from a variety of sources: my own experiences as a business and community leader; the wisdom gained from valued mentors, friends, and family; reading other intelligent and inspiring authors; attending seminars and listening to outstanding speakers. Now that I think about it, the book is actually more of a distillation rather than just a compilation. I want to boil leadership down to its essence - its most important parts - the simple, profound concepts that you can *remember* and *apply.*

Here's one of those profound concepts I offer for you to consider. Through life's experiences I now understand that I don't understand. Knowing that I know that I *don't* know actually brings me peace. Read that again and think about that for a minute. None of us fully understand. None of us knows what all we don't know. We are always learning and discovering. So please know this…it isn't only "just OK" not to be able to explain everything as a leader. It's also freeing to not be burdened with feeling like we have to.

However, I *do* know some things that I believe are worth passing along to you. So please join me and come along for the ride through these pages and be free to lead even though you may not yet fully understand and that there will be unanswered questions for all of us.

THE 4 CORNERSTONES
AND THE
CAPSTONE

For now we see in a mirror, dimly, but then we will see face to face. Now I know only in part; then I will know fully, even as I have been fully known.

– Paul, the Apostle

CHAPTER 1

ALL THINGS ARE NOT AS THEY APPEAR TO BE

Imagine your arms stretched out to either side as wide as you can make them. Wide. Really Wide. My guess is that your hands are a little behind your shoulders. That's about the size of our so-called comfort zone when we were very young. No one had kicked sand in our faces yet. No one had made fun of our thick glasses or the color of our hair or skin. No one had told you how fat/skinny/stupid/slow/unpopular you were yet. Instead, we found ourselves in the dirt or in the doll house or in the woods or in the kitchen where we played unashamedly and unaware of our unlimited imaginations. Remember those blankets secured by heavy books on the coffee tables, chairs, and footstools of our living rooms that made for wonderful tents or caves? Did you ever sleep in yours? How about the free throws you shot into the hoop mounted in the driveway that won come-from-behind victories and made you the hero! And then there was the make-up and hair-do and the princess costume all of which made for a perfect reflection in the mirror.

Yes, our comfort zone was limitless. Until…

Until that little beautiful red-headed girl in first grade wouldn't let you hold her hand. Or you moved to a new town and left all your friends behind. Or you were cut from the basketball team in 8th grade. Or he broke up with you after your senior year. Or your mom left. Or your dad came home drunk and angry again. Or… you fill in the blank.

Slowly, but surely, our comfort zone shrank from being as big as the whole wide world to that of a small object you can easily hold in your hand. In fact, it's about the size of a broken heart.[5]

We've all had our hearts broken in some fashion. Perhaps one small nick at a time that chipped away at us. Perhaps it was one devastating event. Regardless of what the causes may be, if we are honest with ourselves, we need our hearts back. We need to be renewed, restored, refreshed.

We can experience that renewal and restoration and refreshment if we realize that *all things are not as they appear to be.* It is true that there is almost always *more* to a situation than we realize. To illustrate I'll share two stories with you here.

Ron was a friend of ours who was blind from birth. We didn't meet him until late in his life which is when we discovered that he was a champion wrestler in high school as well as a talented pianist. I listened to him play many times and was always amazed at his talent. He also operated several successful enterprises. So even though he couldn't physically see he was a man of vision and accomplishment.

Ron had a wonderful guide dog named Cinder. One day Ron and Cinder came to an intersection controlled by a traffic light. Somehow, Cinder mistakenly led Ron into the oncoming traffic. Miraculously, after dodging cars whose tires were screeching as brakes were slammed on, both dog and man made it safely across the street. When they did, Ron pulled a big dog treat out of his pocket and was about to give it to Cinder. A bystander who had seen all this cried out "Wait! That dog nearly got you killed! Now you're about to reward him with a dog biscuit?!"

Ron excitedly but calmly replied "Yes, I am about to give him this treat. But, you see, *all things are not as they appear to be.* I'm giving him this treat so I can find his mouth because I'm about to kick him in the tail!" Now there's a funny example of discovering that there was *more* to the story.

The other story, which isn't funny at all, took place in the multi-story office building where our business was housed. Our company occupied the top floor of the building and I would often greet people on the elevator who worked for other companies on other floors. One morning I got on the elevator and gave my best "how-do-you-do" to a lady who I recognized, but really didn't know. She didn't acknowledge my greeting in any way. She got off on her floor without looking at me or saying a word and I went on to our floor. Her lack of response didn't set well with me.

When I got off the elevator I was greeted by our talented receptionist. I said good morning, described the woman on the elevator, and asked if she knew her. She told me that she not only knew her, but that they were good friends. I haughtily said "well you need to tell your friend to be a little friendlier in the morning as she just totally ignored me in the elevator." Our receptionist, normally very reserved and perhaps a bit intimidated by me, boldly sat up straight and said " Well, Mr. Miller since she was diagnosed with 4th stage cancer late yesterday afternoon maybe she just doesn't feel like saying much of anything to anybody!"

I felt about an inch tall. See how my perspective changed once I discovered that there was *more* to the story? You can believe that I approached the lady with an entirely different attitude after that.

So back to this comfort zone thing and how it is related to the concept of *more*. When we are nudged, sometimes not so gently, or even forced out of our comfort zone we normally don't like it. Change usually takes us out of our comfort right? A new job (will I succeed?); a new boss (will I measure up?); a new baby (will I be a good parent?); a different policy (what was wrong with the old way of doing things?); a cut in the budget (how will we ever survive?); a death of a loved one (how can I go on without them?). Any of these situations can make us uncomfortable as we adjust and sometimes even grieve our loss of what was.

I've experienced all of the above and confess that initially I didn't appreciate any of them. Yet, with time, the *more* became apparent and, as crazy as it may seem, I now appreciate and have grown because of the lack of comfort. In fact real growth, real maturity, real transformation happens only when we get out of our comfort zones.

May I share two other stories about how being outside my comfort zone transformed my life? First, let me say that the meaning of the word *transform* has a different meaning to me than the word *change*. For example, I may change my clothes each day. I may change the lightbulb in the lamp. I may change the password to my computer. But to transform something or someone is *more* than that. The prefix "trans" means across (such as across time or space or boundaries). The word "form" can mean to shape, to mold, to chisel. For me, being transformed means that, over time, I become different.

I mentioned earlier we are sometimes nudged and sometimes forced out of our comfortable place. This story is about how I was "nudged" over a period of five years to make a significant decision that was quite uncomfortable. It is also the story of why I am able to be writing to you today.

I had the privilege of investing 34 years of my life in the medical equipment industry, the last 20 years with The MED Group, where I served as president and CEO. The company had been headquartered in a Chicago suburb but when I became president we moved the company to my hometown of Lubbock, Texas. We saw MED grow from 27 locations to over 800 in those two decades.

Sometime during the winter of 1999, I had begun to bear the weight of a serious business problem. During a time of quiet reflection with God (which were and still are all too rare I must confess), I cried out "what am I supposed to do?" Almost instantly an inner voice said to me "just walk away and I'll take care of you."

Walk away? Me? No way! I'm no quitter! And walk away from what? The company? The problem? The person causing the problem? Well, it didn't take long to realize what God wanted of me. He wanted me to leave the career I loved...the position and all its trappings of success...the team that I had built. We were making a nice living. I was able to travel in style with my wife, Jayne Ann. I had a retirement plan and insurance benefits and a dependable vehicle. Most importantly to me, The MED Group had a ministry. We were touching the lives of physically challenged people all over the United States. But, despite all of this, the voice would not go away..."Just walk away and I'll take care of you."

One day after speaking at a staff meeting, I was eating dinner in my home when the doorbell rang. I went to see who was at the door, but no one was there. I looked down and on my doorstep were two copies of the book *The Sacred Romance*[6] by John Eldredge and Brent Curtis. Attached was a note which read, "I enjoyed your comments during our staff meeting today. Hope you and your son, Matt, enjoy this book." It was not until many years later I was able to discover who had left that book. I'm still grateful for his thoughtfulness to this day.

Timing is everything and the timing for me receiving this book was perfect. As I read the book and underlined, highlighted, and dog-eared the pages, I continued to hear "just walk away and I'll take care of you." All the while, I was still plugging along the same path in our business endeavors. But soon after, another friend gave me another Eldredge book, *Wild at Heart*[7]. To be honest it sat for a while on the corner of my desk. I couldn't get into it because it spent a lot of pages addressing the "father wound" which I was (and still am) unable to identify with.

However, I skipped over to chapter 11 titled "An Adventure to Live". And when I did the book captured me. The words that really grabbed me were these attributed by Eldredge to Gil Bailie: "Don't ask yourself what the world needs. Ask yourself what makes you come alive, and go do that, because what the world needs is people who have come alive.[8]" It became crystal clear that the voice which had been haunting me to "walk away" was really telling me to pursue my passion…speaking, coaching, mentoring others.

So I closed the book, made a flight reservation to Chicago, and made an appointment to meet there with our board of directors and key investors. I gave them my resignation as head of our company. I told them about the voice and how I had struggled with the decision for the past five years, fully expecting them to "accept my resignation with regrets" and politely ask me to leave. Instead, less than an hour into the meeting they asked me to stay on as chairman of the board with the same pay and benefits until I could discover what I was going to do. And then they offered to buy a portion of my stock to give me seed money for whatever it was I was seeking to do.

I was bowled over. For *five years* I kept saying "No…later… maybe one day…are you kidding?" Yet it took *less than an hour* for God to keep his end of the bargain by taking care of all our concerns about finances, health insurance, stock ownership, and well, everything else.

I returned home and the national search for my replacement began. Later that year (it was now August, 2004), I was in Colorado Springs at the beautiful Broadmoor Resort for a meeting with a group of clients. By that time we had found my replacement as CEO. As I awoke that morning I prayed and asked "What am I supposed to do now? I need to start my new life, but what is it I am supposed to do?" In answer to my prayer that still small voice said "Make a plan."

With that answer I became angry. "Make a plan to do what? I did what you asked. I walked away. Now what?" And the voice, always so tender and soft said "Make a plan." Frustrated, I went to the meeting. I'm glad I wasn't facilitating that day because surprisingly thoughts came to me about a plan so fast that the ink would hardly flow fast enough from my pen. I wrote down ideas about a place…a place where men, primarily corporate executives like me, could get their hearts back…a place where they could be refreshed and have their spirits renewed. I imagined a place where they could be little boys again "playing in the dirt"…a place where they could ride, shoot, climb, jump, laugh…without any fear of failure or rebuke.

I thought about the importance of teams of men working together and how this place would coach teams to be stronger by working in unity. This place would exercise and teach servant leadership and would encompass humility, authenticity, and passion for its mission. It would be a place of spiritual awakening. Yet it would not be a "churchy" place with yelling from a pulpit or Bible thumping or guilt producing comments from others. In other words it would be a safe place to be genuine and vulnerable and strong.

Soon after I decided that this place would have a western, ranch-style feel to it. Since in West Texas we don't have majestic mountains (no joke!), pristine lakes, or piney woods then the ranch concept fits. Because what we do have are rodeos, cattle, ranchers, farmers, oil, and cotton. So cattle, horses, spurs and cowboy hats filled my imagination. The only problem…I wasn't a cowboy. Heck, I didn't know the front end from the back end of a horse. And then, where is this ranch going to be? I sure didn't own one nor could I afford to buy one.

Since graduating from Monterey High School in Lubbock, Texas in 1967, 12 friends have stuck together. Beginning with our 21st graduation anniversary we have gone on a retreat together every year. During a conversation with one of those friends, Steve Hurt[9], I told the "walk away" saga and described my vision for the ranch. He asked the same question I had been asking…where will it be? A few weeks later Steve shared the story with another one of the 12, Randy Andrews[10] and he asked me "So, what about this ranch? Where will it be?" This question was beginning to sound way too familiar. He then floored me when he offered one of his properties north of Lubbock that was perfect for our new venture. This was another example of God "taking care of me" by providing 250 acres with buildings, horse facilities, and the prettiest scenery in the county.

The stories within this story go on and on. How the name of "the place" became Spirit Ranch. How I met our co-founder, James Cutrera. How a real cowboy was brought into our lives giving us expertise with our livestock. How Mariano Villalobos would turn his life around and become our trusted jack-of-all trades. How as a part-time college student Michelle Cook became our general manager and our rock. How working on a shoestring month after month turned into trusting that somehow money would be made available. And it always was.

We put a lot of thought and planning into what Spirit Ranch would be. Even with all that planning and the work of our team, we laughed at how much those plans changed. I had said from the beginning that we were going to abide by a strict "men only" and "no kids" curriculum. In the ten years that Spirit Ranch was hosting guests from businesses, schools, governmental agencies, churches, and families we had over 30,000 people come through our gates for team and leadership development. Of those, over half were women and over 5,000 were students ranging from 3rd grade through medical school. As they say "men make plans and God laughs."

I'm no longer with Spirit Ranch and the reason is the basis for my next story. It's another example of how there is always *more* to our stories.

Life is like an ice cream cone.
You have to lick it one day at a time.

– Charlie Brown of *Peanuts*

CHAPTER 2

YES. THERE REALLY *IS* MORE

She died. Even after all this time since then it's still difficult to say those words. Jayne Ann lost her war with lymphoma on September 1, 2012. We were married for 40 years, 2 months and 29 days. That's 14,701 days if you count the extra days of the leap years in those four decades. That's a lot of days! Did we have some bad days? Sure. But the good days outnumbered the bad ones many times over. I'm breaking a promise I made to her by telling you how courageous and strong and everything good she was during her illness. She didn't want to have people think any more highly of her than she actually was. Well, I'm here to tell you she actually *was* courageous, strong, and everything good. And the legacy she left is inscribed with her name on an elementary school, a sorority chapter hall, at her alma mater Texas Tech, student scholarships, and the hearts of all who loved her.

Jayne Ann never asked "why me?" But I did. I asked in no uncertain terms "why her?" Why us? Why our family and our children and grandchildren? Why now? Why so much pain? Her answer, although somewhat jumbled by her pain medication, was "why *not* me" She told people that she wasn't exempt from such suffering in the world and that, one way or the other, everything would work out. Well, it did work out, but not in the way that I wanted.

The very first get well card she received was from our son, Tim. It is now framed and sits in his office where he practices as a gastroenterologist. The card says "One day, one step at a time." I learned after she left us that many times it was one *moment*, one *breath* at a time. I was overwhelmed with our loss and often felt as though I was in a fog. I became clumsy and inattentive. I hurt for our kids and their kids. And while I like being alone now and then I didn't like being lonely at all. And there is a big difference in the two.

Four months after losing Jayne Ann, Bob McKelvy, a mentor/friend of mine died. Although he was almost 20 years older than me, we had been friends with him and his wife, Maxine, for many years. Naturally I attended his memorial service. At the reception that day I noticed a beautiful lady standing next to the widow. When I asked about her I found out that she was my friends' daughter, Katherine, who I had never met. Because I was still in that "fog" and far from ready to begin a new relationship I didn't meet her that day. But, I will admit I *did* notice her!

About six months later I was pretty sure I saw her in the grocery store. So, I took a deep breath and introduced myself. Sure enough it was Katherine. We chatted briefly and when I said that I should take her mother out to dinner for a visit, she offered to "chaperone". Well, I didn't even get the hint. She wanted to get to know more about me. Not too sharp am I? Another year went by and I was ready to at least put my toe in the dating waters so I asked her out to dinner. After five hours of dining and conversation I was highly impressed (to say the least).

We dated (that sounds so high-schoolish!) for the next two years. We needed the time to not only get to know each other well, but to work through our own situations before being ready to wed. Gratefully, I am glad to tell you that on October 1, 2016 Katherine and I married and established our home in Horseshoe Bay, Texas. The joy we have experienced has been wonderful and I can't imagine life without her.

More. There is almost always *more*! Therefore, not all things are as they appear to be. What may be true today could be the altered truth in the future. It is still true that I'm no longer the CEO of a company, but I am delighted and fulfilled to be a leadership coach. And it is true that Jayne Ann is no longer with her loved ones, but Katherine has offered a bright light in our lives that illuminates hope and joy and love.

So as we navigate the chapters that follow be on the lookout for the *more* in your life. I believe you will soon discover that all things are not as they appear to be and that the best lies ahead of us.

If you build it, they will come.

– Field of Dreams

CHAPTER 3

THE FOUR CORNERSTONES AND THE CAPSTONE

The term "cornerstone" while used traditionally in reference to the construction of a structure, is also often used metaphorically to describe something that is dependable, stable, and an integral part of something significant. I've used the cornerstone term as a visual tool allowing others to relate to foundational truth. Whether building a house, marriage, partnership, company, church, or school a solid foundation is essential. If we ignore the strength of the foundation we can count on the eventuality of the overall structure being damaged, even destroyed.

The "capstone" is the final stone laid as a construction project comes to completion. It represents the culmination of achievement. Some would say it is the greatest part of something. And it is obvious that the capstone cannot be placed unless the foundation and the remainder of the structure has been completed. Using the capstone term in leadership development is the result of successfully laying and maintaining the sturdiness of the cornerstones.

The image comes from the ancient quarries where highly-trained stonemasons carefully chose the stones used in construction. No stone was more important than the cornerstone because the integrity of the whole structure depended on the cornerstone containing exactly the right lines. If the cornerstone was not exactly right, the entire building would be out of line. For that reason, builders inspected many stones, rejecting each one until they found the one they wanted. Rejected stones might be used in other parts of the building, but they would never become the cornerstone or the capstone (the first and last stones put in place).[11]

In our work at Spirit Ranch we learned much more from the leaders we hosted than they learned from us. The insights they shared from their experiences were invaluable in shaping what I call the four cornerstones and the capstone. As I mentioned in the introduction, much is owed to the many leadership authors and speakers for their wisdom. So much, in fact, that I find myself overwhelmed by the quantity of it all. Thus, the reason for my desire to extract and distill the essential and most important aspects of leadership for us to apply.

There are four cornerstones that will help organizations and individuals succeed. These four principles are commonly known but not commonly practiced. If applied, they will help guide you as a leader in your organization and home through the choppy waters of challenges and changes. The laying and proper maintenance of these cornerstones will also lead to the crowning achievement of placing the capstone in its rightful place. That capstone is very simply...well read on. I will describe all of the stones briefly here and then go into detail in the following chapters.

The first cornerstone is *trust*. Every relationship whether personal or corporate begins and thrives with trust. Broken trust damages or ends those relationships. Therefore, trust is the cornerstone that must be laid first. As vital as the other stones are they cannot get in front of this one. And, the trust cornerstone has to be revisited often as we examine "what went wrong?" or "how can we improve?" In fact, all four cornerstones need to be laid in the correct sequence and they also will be constantly reviewed in an almost circuitous fashion. Just remember that until and unless all the key elements of trust are in place, everything else will either have to be put on hold or will simply limp along.

The second cornerstone to be laid, assuming again that trust has or is being achieved, is that of *understanding*. I used to use the term "communication" to describe this component of leadership but found out that far too often communication was being transmitted but not received. One example is the used of the alphabet soup of acronyms that every industry has. If you talk to a non-financial person about EBITDA or COGS or LTV[12] they may nod their head as though they understand because they're too embarrassed to let you know that they don't. Different languages, remote offices, time zones, and false assumptions are just a few of the barriers that cause problems with truly understanding each other.

Assuming that trust and understanding are firmly in place we go to the third cornerstone, *freedom*. I don't know if it's just me or if others would agree with me, but I just love this cornerstone. It is empowering! Usually we think if we empower someone we give them authority or permission to do something. Let me give you some other words that are not as frequently used to define empowerment. How about set free; give freedom; emancipate[13]. Too often we are *not* free to do what ought to be done. But when trust and understanding have been established then we are, indeed, given freedom! I find that exciting!

The last cornerstone follows in order and, like the capstone, is a result of the others being in their place. This is the cornerstone of *unity*. Oh my, the power of being unified can be immeasurable. Of course, the opposite is true, too. A lack of unity leads to places we would rather not go. And just to make sure I'm clear, I'm not speaking here of uniformity where we all dress, act, and talk alike. And, I'm not addressing unanimity which demands that we are all in perfect agreement on every decision. Instead, being united means that in spite of our differences we are all pulling on the same rope in the same direction for a cause that is greater than any one of us.

Finally, if we have all the cornerstones firmly set in their places we are ready to lay the capstone. I suppose a drum roll isn't necessary but the feeling that people get when they realize that they have earned the privilege of placing the capstone is truly special. The capstone is *joy*. And who wouldn't want to live in a home or work in a business or learn in a school or worship in a church or serve in a government where joy exists! I know places that are devoid of joy and others that are overflowing with it. The productivity and profitability of the latter are immensely greater than those of the former.

There are four key elements to every cornerstone that I'll visit with you about in each cornerstone's chapter. If any one of these four elements is missing then most likely that cornerstone is not carrying its portion of the foundational load. As a leader you can examine each element and diagnose a problem quickly. Let's take a look at each cornerstone and their elements in greater detail in the chapters ahead.

We often think trust is *built by grand gestures at crucial moments in our lives, but trust is typically built with simplicity and small actions. It's very clear. Trust is built in very small moments.*

– Brene Brown

CHAPTER 4

THE TRUST CORNERSTONE

For most of my life I believed that trust simply involved being honest. Mutual trust was to be developed based on truth telling. Of course, I still believe that honesty is the best policy, but trust involves so much more than just that. Let me explain by describing the trust cornerstone elements.

Wholeheartedness

The first element is *wholeheartedness.* If we are to be wholehearted then we must be men and women of integrity. Integrity is closely related to another term we all learned in elementary math class...integer. Remember back to our math classes that a fraction is part of a number (1/2, 2/3, 1/8) while an integer is a whole number (9, 78, 436)? If something is fractured it has been divided or separated (like a fraction). Or you might think of the contrast between integrated and segregated. The former indicates the whole while the latter defines being divided.

So if we are wholehearted it means we are giving our whole selves...not just our honesty, but also our creativity, effort, teamsmanship, loyalty, devotion, work ethic. A wholehearted person is bold to stand up and speak when they believe strongly about an issue. Yet, they are wise enough to stay silent when silence would win the day. A wholehearted leader is "giving it all they've got".

Now here's an important question. If I'm giving my whole self at work or in my community as a volunteer, what am I going to have left to give my family…those that matter most to me? Just as you would not leave on a long distance trip with the needle on your gas gauge nearing empty, you shouldn't go home with an "empty tank" either. This is where wisdom comes into play and the practice of appropriately saying "no" will help you. You have to leave enough energy inside to not only show up at home, but be wholehearted there as well.

So, the question we must ask ourselves is "Am I a person… a leader…that is giving all I've got? Am I giving my whole self to the cause; to the people I lead and serve; to the people I live with? If not, then I must ask myself what I can do to become whole again. Interesting challenge to lead with "whole-heartedness isn't it?

Competence

I'm giving serious consideration to auditioning on The Voice soon. After that I thought trying out for the United States Olympic hockey team would be interesting. And to make sure I'm setting my goals high enough I plan to take up watercolor so I can get a piece of my art in the Washington's National Gallery of Art.

Ludicrous you say? Yes, indeed. And the reason is you can't trust me to succeed at any of the three plans. I may be wholehearted in my efforts. But I lack the second element of *competence* and therefore can't be trusted to deliver.

What if a person where you work or live with is of the highest integrity…giving you all he's got; never lying to you; always on time; courteous; creative; a team player? And what if that same person agrees completely with you on the direction you need to go on a project or task or strategy and who should be responsible for which elements of your endeavor? And yet, they can never seem to finish their work on time, on budget, on target.

What's missing? Could it be a lack of competence? And the person may actually have the capability to do the job as you'd like but they don't have the proper training or education or enough experience or the wrong supervisor. What then? Mentor them. Coach them up. Or, put them in another position where they can succeed and contribute to the organization. Expand on what they *can* do rather than continuing to ask them to perform at a level for which they are not equipped.

Yes, there are those instances where you are going to have to terminate the employee who ultimately just doesn't "get it." Continuing to ask for high level performance from a person not geared for that position is defeating for both the organization and the individual. Move them over or move them out today.

Alignment

The next trust element which Stephen M.R. Covey describes in his book *The Speed of Trust*[14] is "intention". I call it the *alignment* of leaders and their team members. Imagine train tracks that are *almost* parallel. When you measure the distance between them up close they seem to be "ok". Just ok? In a matter of minutes as the train makes it way down the track those track rails are going to get further and further apart so that ultimately…well, you get the picture. We would have a train wreck on our hands.

Let's assume that you and your co-worker (or family member or fellow volunteer) are both wholehearted…persons of integrity; therefore, you have no doubt that the other is telling the truth and giving a 100% effort. But, what if their agenda is different from yours? That difference is not necessarily good or bad (although it certainly can be in some instances)…it's just different. Such a difference could lead to your own kind of train wreck.

When Southwest Airlines first launched, it implemented a love potion theme. All flight attendants dressed in love-associated costumes and passed out "love potions" and "love bites," which later became known as drinks and peanuts. When Southwest Airlines was listed on the New York Stock Exchange it chose the ticker symbol LUV because of the company's love potion beginnings.[15]

I luv Southwest Airlines and their "bags-fly-free" policy. Nothing wrong with American, Delta, United, and other airlines that are charging to fly your luggage. On the one hand, Southwest has turned this contrast into a huge positive public relations campaign for their business resulting in more passengers, thus, more revenue. On the other hand, the other airlines have increased their revenue from baggage fees. Which solution is best? Both are good positions. Both have potentially positive and negative outcomes. Both are honest and ethical approaches to the issue.

Now just imagine this. Let's say I check in for a Southwest flight in Austin, Texas (which I often do). I'm warmly greeted and when the ticket agent checks my bag there is no additional fee. I walk away smiling. But, what if on the return portion of my trip I check in at, let's say, Atlanta and the ticket agent warmly greets me and tells me that I owe $25.00 for my checked bag. What?!?! That's not the policy of SWA. But apparently one agent at one airport is aligned with the company policy and the other agent at another airport is not. Now…can I trust Southwest in the future if this becomes a regular occurrence? No, I cannot because there is a lack of alignment. By the way, I in fact to trust Southwest because my bags fly free no matter where I check them in.

So ultimately, whatever policy you adopt or decision you make or market you enter or product you develop, unless and until you and your associates agree on being aligned, a full degree of trust doesn't exist. Why? Because you are pursuing one route and the other person is pursuing another causing counter-productivity and, at best, mixed results. So, the team members' goals must be brought into alignment before a plan is launched.

Production

Production is the fourth and final "element of credibility" Covey writes about in *The Speed of Trust*. The term he uses in the book is "results". Like a car with only three good tires, trust requires this fourth element to give you a "smooth ride".

I know a gentleman who was hired as the head of a national company in the health care business. The firm was almost 20 years old at the time but was floundering in debt, shrinking revenues, diminished customer confidence, and a product line that was meager. Yet there was a certain spirit about the organization that sent a subtle message that, with the right people, attitudes, effort, and blessing, things could be turned around.

So, on a cold winter January day this new CEO and a lean staff dedicated themselves and the business to the highest in standards: ethics, effort, creativity, communication, and…of course, trust. They did so to honor their customers, but also to strive for extraordinary production for all stakeholders.

While the CEO had demonstrated his wholehearted efforts over the years to the stockholders of this company, he also learned and became aligned with their goals so that their intentions were the same. Fortunately, his track record had already proven that he had the competence needed to be hired in the first place. But, those that hired him could not fully trust him in those early months. Why not? Because he had yet to produce any results for them.

By surrounding himself with capable, hard-working, innovative folks (yes, trustworthy people you might conclude), they were able to deliver well above the expected return on investment which more than satisfied all stakeholders.

During the years that followed losses became handsome profits; the product line became the envy of the industry; people blossomed; customers benefited; cash flow paid off all debt; and the stock value of the company soared. Then and only then...<u>after</u> they had performed and produced outstanding results, were the CEO and his team fully trusted. FYI that CEO was yours truly.

So there you have it. Trust requires:

- Wholeheartedness
- Alignment
- Competence
- Production

How are you doing in developing trusting relationships? Ponder the following questions and answer them wholeheartedly.

Would the people you live or work with say that you are living with integrity and giving your full effort?

When you know someone else is not being wholehearted how do you approach the situation?

How do handle situations when people have not been able to prove their competence in a given area?

Where are you lacking in competency and what are you doing about it?

What are you continually doing to make certain that you are aligned with those you work or live with?

What gets measured gets done. What are you measuring that proves you're achieving expected results?

He who cherishes understanding prospers. Understanding is a fountain of life to those who have it. Though it cost all you have, get understanding.

– Solomon

CHAPTER 5

THE UNDERSTANDING CORNERSTONE

Regardless of the size, type, longevity, or location of the organizations I get to work with, the number one problem I consult on is this: disappointments caused by misunderstandings due to unclear expectations. There are so many examples I could site. Such as..."you said *this* week? I thought you said *next* week." Or...but Mom said my curfew was midnight and now you're telling me it's 11:00?" How about..."The shipment was to have included the freight charges, but now they've added extra for them."

Can you think of a few examples of your own? Most likely you won't have to go back more than a few hours to recall some. Why is this? How can things get so messed up when they seem so simple? My response is that we don't lean on the understanding cornerstone nearly enough.

Discovering

Understanding starts with *discovery.* Getting information. Learning. And there are so many ways we discover things. We can search the internet. Watch a documentary. Listen to a podcast. Attend a seminar. Sit in on a meeting. Touch a hot stove. Smell bacon frying. Go on an adventure. Show up and work hard. Pay attention. You name some more ways we learn and absorb information.

Of all these methods I believe that empathic listening…listening to truly understand…is both the most impactful and the most neglected. It seems like actively listening to another person should come so naturally. But with all the distractions around us and inside our minds, good listeners are rare. Empathic listening is a learned skill and anyone who puts some effort into it can become proficient.

Think about the benefits of active listening. Increased productivity. Achievement of goals. Reduction of misunderstandings. Setting the stage for "the next thing". Soothing or healing relationships. Considering new ideas and questioning assumptions. Showing appreciation and respect. And yet within two months we remember less than 25% of what we've heard and we may forget a third to a half of what we heard only 8 hours ago.[16] We all need to become a better listener. Doing so includes why we listen; becoming an active listener; realizing what people say about poor listeners; and barriers you may face when listening. For now just keep in mind that a lack of discovery through poor listening habits is where misunderstandings begin.

An example we could use throughout this cornerstone could be this. Let's say a man (me) called home to let his wife know that he is leaving work at 6:15pm and will be home for dinner that evening. Was his wife actively listening? See the elements that follow for the answer.

Clarifying

Clarifying information that we receive reminds me of a hilarious video of my 2-year old grandson. He (and his mother) had just experienced the long-awaited victory of him going pee-pee in the potty. So, mom decided to video his reaction/celebration after being rewarded with some M&M's. In it she asks "did you go pee-pee in the potty?" and over and over again he exclaimed in that little toddler voice "I pee potty! I pee potty! I pee potty!" At the end of the short video there was no doubt that he had peed in the potty. Why? Because he had clarified what his mother had said.

Repeating or parroting what has been communicated to us, whether verbally or in writing, is the second element in reaching understanding. You are clarifying what has been said by simply recalling the other person's words to them. If you've repeated their words accurately they will acknowledge that you have heard them correctly. If not, this is the perfect time to make a correction.

Using our example from the discovery element above, the wife could have repeated what the man (me) said. She was thinking that he said he'd be home for dinner at 6:15. But she didn't say what she was thinking. Instead she simply said something like this. "Please be on time because I want everything out of the oven and off the stove at just the right time for you." Just FYI, the man (me) said, "OK." Hhhmmm....I smell trouble in the air, do you?

Questioning

The next step in truly understanding is *asking questions*. You're not challenging the other person or their ideas. You are simply asking for more information or requesting an alternative thought. Challenging will come later under the freedom cornerstone. Let's say you just moved from one of your company's cities to another and there is a different PTO policy. You had already planned on taking time away from work that would have been allowed under your previous location's policy, but not under the new one. So, having clarified with your new manager what the policy states, you ask if you could have a one-time exception so that you can follow through with your previous plans. It's just a question. Your manager may say yes or no, but at least you asked the question.

Remember before we are working on this cornerstone the first one of trust has already been laid. At the current moment there is a mutual trust. And you want to make sure you are staying in alignment and building that trust. So I want to repeat that for the sake of establishing or maintaining good relationships with those around you this is not the time to complain or criticize, whine or gripe. It is not the time to challenge the policy or idea or person either. Such a challenge should only come about after both trust and understanding have been established.

Now, back to our dinner example. The man (me) said he would *leave work* at 6:15 and be home for dinner. His wife was thinking, but didn't say that he would *be home* at 6:15. Instead of clarifying the time she just made the request that he (I) be on time. He (I) said "OK." What if a question had been asked by either party in this case now? Oh, yeah…trouble is definitely on its way.

Confirming

This is the final step in reaching an agreed upon understanding. You've discovered some information. You've clarified it by repeating it. You've asked questions about it. And now you are read to *confirm* what you've agreed to. In the world of distractions and the whirlwind of activity around us it is no wonder that we disappoint one another because we didn't really understand. That's why we have contracts and leases and invoices and other transactional documents. It's why we need to confirm almost everything in writing.

Not necessarily because we don't trust the other person. Remember, trust is already in place. But, we may not remember the conversation later and we need to be able to refer to a document to jog our memories.

Email…blessing or curse? There's a subject for another day! But in this case sending and acknowledging emails that confirm our understanding can be invaluable to us. After a conversation (in person, on the phone, in a meeting, or on a teleconference) a summary of what was said is always helpful. A written company policy is almost always better than a verbal one. Contracts and Memorandums of Understanding give clarity and confirmation to the handshake of understanding.

How did things go at dinner that fateful night? Not so good I'm afraid. I got home and she was hot but the food was not! I asked what the matter was. She replied that I had told her I'd be home at 6:15. I rebutted by saying "no I said that I was leaving work at 6:15. It's a 15 minute drive from work to home so you should have expected me at 6:30. In fact, it's not quite 6:30 yet so I'm actually early." She then told me that the least I could do was be on time after all the work she had put in on preparing the meal. (Side note: this is my sweet late wife and she really had worked hard preparing dinner). So to make her feel better I said "Well, no big deal since I can rewarm it in the microwave." (Yes, I am an idiot sometime.)

About a week later when she was speaking to me again (just kidding about it being a week…it was only 5 days), we talked about how wrong things had gone that day. Being the leadership

Everything that is really great and inspiring is created by the individual who can labor in freedom.

– Albert Einstein

CHAPTER 6

THE FREEDOM CORNERSTONE

Without the cornerstones of trust and understanding preceding, we cannot experience the freedom that I'm describing below. But if those two are in place then people sense the empowerment they have for the following elements.

I cite the two following examples to illustrate the first element of the freedom cornerstone...*innovation and failure*. Imagine where we would be today without the many "failures" of inventors, scientists, and adventurers. I can't think of a single product that I use today that didn't have a predecessor of failure. The vehicles we drive. The airplanes we fly in. The computers we use. The refrigerators that preserve our food. The list is endless.

Don't you enjoy hearing the history of the Post-it® Note?[17] I've read the story many times and have told it on countless occasions. Dr. Spencer Silver, a 3M scientist, was busily researching adhesives in the laboratory. In the process, he discovered something peculiar: an adhesive that stuck lightly to surfaces but didn't bond tightly to them. For years, Silver struggled to find a use for his invention. But that didn't keep him from touting the merits of his creation to colleagues. "I came to be known as Mr. Persistent because I wouldn't give up."

Meanwhile, Art Fry, another 3M scientist, was frustrated.

Every Wednesday night while practicing with his church choir, he would use little scraps of paper to mark the hymns they were going to sing in the upcoming service. By Sunday, he'd find that they'd all fallen out of the hymnal. He needed a bookmark that would stick to the paper without damaging the pages. Fry and Silver put their heads together and the story of the little yellow sticky pad continues.

Post-it® Notes are now available in more than 150 countries. Collectively, there are more than 4,000 Post-it® Products. Having seen Post-it® Notes featured in films, mosaic pop art and the daily lives of millions, Dr. Silver is blown away. "The fact that they've just exploded as a product is more than I could ever hope for."

The story of Thomas Edison's persistence in perfecting the incandescent light bulb is legend, as well. Thomas Edison was one of the most successful innovators in American history. He was the "Wizard of Menlo Park," a larger-than-life hero who seemed almost magical for the way he snatched ideas from thin air. But the man also stumbled, sometimes tremendously. In response to a question about his missteps, Edison once said, "I have not failed 10,000 times—I've successfully found 10,000 ways that will not work."[18]

Regardless of the product or idea, an environment that encourages creativity and experimentation is essential. And along with that environment came the understanding that some things are not going to work. There will be mistakes, overextended budgets, and failures. But it's ok. We are free to experiment and fail because we have trust and understanding with one another.

Next on the list of elements for freedom is *challenge*. Remember (again) we have established trust meaning we are working with people of integrity and competence who are in alignment with each other as they produce the work at hand. And, we have a clear understanding of our objectives and tasks because we have communicated well and clarified, questioned, and confirmed our expectations. And, only now are we free to challenge one another regardless of title or position.

There was an instance at Spirit Ranch during which I wanted us to adopt the highway that ran next to our property. The purpose was to partner with the highway department to keep litter cleaned up on the roadsides. It was a two mile stretch and I thought it would be both neighborly and a good public relations thing to do. And, I believe we could recruit volunteers to do the actual work.

Michelle, our general manager who reported directly to me, challenged the idea and expressed some valid reservations. She was opposed to the clean-up project for a number of reasons. The discussion became rather frustrating and a little heated before I insisted that we move forward with the adopt-a-highway program.

Two points to be made. One, our GM didn't hesitate to challenge me, her "boss", because we had built a wonderful relationship based on trust and a common mission. We did our best to create an atmosphere where people were not afraid to speak their minds. Two, I was dead wrong about the project. After only a few months we abandoned the highway clean-up for the exact reasons that Michelle had voiced earlier. Fortunately, I was free to fail…not only in relation to the project itself, but in being hard-headed to begin with.

It is important to note here that we are not free to challenge others in such a way that demeans or discourages or belittles them. Challenge the idea or the thought process or the data.

Know that it is alright to debate the issues that come before us...strongly if needed. But, if it becomes necessary to address character issues, that is to be done privately and professionally.

Innovation and Failure. Challenge. The third element of freedom is that of *ownership*. I used to use the word accountability here and I believe strongly in the concept of holding each other accountable. I prefer the use of the word ownership thought because it denotes a high level of responsibility. I will speak first on the need for me to take responsibility for myself and what I have committed to do. I cannot allow myself weak excuses or invalid justifications for not meeting your expectations of me. If I agreed to it, then I must do it.

At the same time, because of the trust and understanding that exists (or should exist) we have the freedom and responsibility to make sure each other is taking ownership of their commitments, too. There are worksheets in the appendix that will help you approach difficult conversations and the gap between what was agreed upon (the expected) and what was performed (the actual). The longer we don't hold each other accountable, the wider the gap grows.

A mental illustration of driving a car comes to mind. As your car begins to drift to one side or the other you almost unconsciously make a minor correction. But if you let the car continue to drift a crisis arises and you have to make a major adjustment which could result in rolling your car or going off into a ditch. The same is true with someone not meeting their performance expectations. The situation rarely gets better on its own so early intervention is vital. Take a look at the "accountability gap" illustration in the appendix.

Finally, we are free to *have fun*! Life is too short (remember my age) to be miserable. We all should find enjoyment in our work. Remember that wise old Solomon said, "There is nothing better for people than to eat and drink, and to find enjoyment in their work."[19]

So now you know that freedom allows:

- Innovation/Failure
- Challenge
- Ownership
- Fun

Give an example of how you encourage innovation.

State how you go about allowing reasonable errors to be made.

Illustrate how much you agree or disagree that your culture permits challenging one another.

How do you hold people accountable for what they've taken ownership of?

And, tell how you give others the right to hold you accountable of your responsibilities.

Tell a story about how work is fun in your environment.

United we stand; divided we fall.
A lion used to prowl about a field in which four oxen used to dwell. Many a time he tried to attack them; but whenever he came near they turned their tails to warn another, so that whichever way he approached them he was met by the horns of one of them. At last, however, they fell a-quarrelling [sic] among themselves, and each went off to pasture alone in the separate corner of the field. Then the Lion attacked them one by one and soon made an end of all four.

- Aesop's Fables

CHAPTER 7

THE UNITY CORNERSTONE

One way to describe the concept of synergy is to think of 1 + 1 = 3. Two good ideas coming together to form a new idea that is even greater than the sum of the parts. That's the way I believe the cornerstone of unity works. Trust + Understanding + Freedom = Something better, stronger, more desirable than any of the other cornerstones standing on their own.

I've often asked myself which cornerstone is the most important. Which is my favorite? If I had to choose only one, which would it be? I can't come up with just one...or two...or three. While I do believe that the four stones should be considered in the order that I've listed them, beginning with trust, I can't find a way to either favor or eliminate even one. It would be like saying which would you rather do without...your neurological system, your respiratory system, your cardiovascular system, or your digestive system? Which one of these is the most important? Your favorite? The answer is "E"...all of the above.

That being said I am enamored with the 4th cornerstone. Probably because it is so...so...so moving. Take a look at these elements and see if they don't stir something in you that seems right and good.

A team, staff, family, military, political party, nation, church, club that is unified stimulates *encouragement*. As I work with groups all across America I find a disturbing fact. That fact is that fear is the number one motivator in our society. It's probably always been that way, but it seems to be escalating in modern times. Fear that I won't measure up. Fear that I won't be included. Fear that I'm not smart enough, tall enough, skinny enough, cool enough, experienced enough. Fear that I'm too slow, too black or white, too late, too old or young. Fear is everywhere and if you don't see it or feel it then rest assured it is lurking just below the surface.

Now there is a healthy kind of fear right? The kind that helps us survive. If I'm afraid because the lion is chasing me then I'm going to run. If I'm afraid because the diagnosis is serious I'm going to do exactly what the doctor says. If I'm afraid she's considering leaving me I'm going to court her all over again. If the enemy is firing at me and I'm afraid for my life I'm going to get in my foxhole and fight back. But, what is the one thing we need the most to respond to such fear?

Courage, that's what. Courage isn't the antidote for fear. But it is what helps us work through the fear. Courage gives us some intangible something that makes us respond with hope and certainty. That something is your heart. The word courage stems from the Latin "cor" and more recently from the old French word "corage". Going back as early as the 13th century translated it means "valor, quality of mind which enables one to meet danger and trouble without fear. Words in Old English for heart are also commonly metaphors for inner strength.[20]

Remember the first element of trust? Wholeheartedness. We will all struggle with be wholehearted, people of integrity, if our hearts are broken or fearful. People working in unity give each other courage within…or we know it as encouragement. By the way would you like to know what the antidote for fear is? It's found in scripture and it is true that *perfect love casts out all fear*. Think about that. Are you afraid of someone that has your back, is always there for you, and loves you no matter what? Not likely! I had a healthy respect for my dad when I was growing up and I knew that I would have to answer to him if I misbehaved. But, I don't have any recollection of fearing him because I knew he loved me with his whole heart. Man I miss him!

The second element of unity is *grace*. Forgiving each other. Cutting some slack. Giving a little space. Having empathy. I've said to groups many times, "Listen. We are all just a bunch of screw-up's and I'm the chief of that bunch." In other words we all make mistakes. We all are going to let someone down now and then. And if we are going to have the freedom to fail as we innovate then we darn sure better be willing to give grace to one another!

Incidentally, there is something a bit irrational about giving and receiving grace. We live in a society that demands a balance between debits and credits. A society that "pays an honest wage for honest work". A society that says if I didn't earn it then I don't deserve it. Here is the irrational part of grace: it is undeserved; it is unearned; it is a gift and is yours for the taking and yours for the giving. There is no charge for grace. And by the way, I know there are way too many exceptions to this. There has always been and there always will be freeloaders. Guess what? They need grace, too.

Element number three comprising the unity cornerstone is *compassion*. Let me assure you that I am not some expert in etymology (the study of words). Or entomology for that matter either (the study of insects). But I do love to dig deeper into the original meanings of words via the search engines on the internet that are available to us. (Remember…seek is part of my mission statement.) So let's take a look at this word compassion.

The prefix "com" means "with or together". The word passion comes from the Latin root "pati" meaning suffering, or enduring. Thus, compassion means to suffer-with. If you stand in unity with someone you are willing to suffer with them. And, conversely if you suffer alongside a person, you will further solidify your unity.

I told you that my wife, Jayne Ann, died in 2012. She was diagnosed with lymphoma some years before then, but her only symptom was an elevated white blood cell count. That was discovered during a routine annual exam. While at first alarming, we were grateful that for several years the oncologists and hematologists prescribed a "watch and wait" regimen. That simply meant that every few months she would have her blood tested to monitor the WBC count. After continuing to rise for the first few checks it returned to perfectly normal levels for almost a year.

Then, in April of 2012, the cancer "blossomed". Jayne Ann would say, "well it's spring time and everything else is blossoming so why not this disease?" I appreciated her humor, but not the blossom. The cancer spread like wildfire into her lymph nodes, her uterus, her breasts. She was put on an extraordinarily heavy chemotherapy cocktail. In and out of the hospital for the next five months she experienced every side-effect that you hear about. Nausea, hair falling out, loss of appetite, weaknesses, etc.

But the two things that really struck the hardest the last seven weeks of her life were the excruciating pain and paralysis caused by the demyelination of all her nervous systems. For the pain she took Tramadol, Morphine, Dilaudid, and Fentanyl. Nothing relieved the pain but eventually the medication mercifully made her sleep. Demyelination results in damage to the protective covering (myelin sheath) that surrounds nerve fibers in your brain, optic nerves and spinal cord. When the myelin sheath is damaged, nerve impulses slow or even stop, causing neurological problems.

Yes indeed neurological problems did exist. She lost her ability to move (motor nervous system). She had no sensation in her touch (sensory nervous system). And she no longer controlled her heart rate, blood pressure, digestive system or urinary system (autonomic nervous system). If she was awake she could communicate although the heavy dosage of pain meds made it difficult. One of my pleasant memories is of a night where all of our kids and her sister, Christine, were with us in her hospital room and we had a great family conversation. I recorded it and have listened to it many times. I love the combination of the laughter and the tears and the stories that we shared all with a Little League World Series game going on in the background on the television.

We were with her the Saturday that she spoke her last word and took her last breath. Three of our young grandkids came to say hello that afternoon. When they came into the room Jayne Ann mumbled to the two girls, "hey there Baby Cakes." That was the last thing we heard her say. Our three adult children and their spouses were there along with my mother and sisters all day. We had agreed well in advance not to administer any life support or resuscitation. Early that evening she slipped away as I laid next to her.

My reason for giving so many details of her illness and death is to let you know about how we all had compassion for each other...how we suffered together. Yes, she was most certainly the one who bore the physical pain and mental anguish. Yet at the same time the rest of us who were closest to her and knew her best suffered too. The emotional strain watching and hearing her hurt was intense. The long nights at the hospital and the travel for some of our family members to see her were exhausting. You may have experienced a similar trial so you know what I'm talking about.

Our family was very close before all of this happened to us. And that bond was only strengthened both during her illness and the grief we shared afterward. It was being unified that allowed that to happen. It doesn't take illness or death to have compassion. You know that. So for the sake of your family and your team and your organization, put all the cornerstones in place and keep working them. The return on the investment of your conscious effort will be significant.

The final element of being unified is *strength.* Aesop's fable on the cover page of this chapter reminds us of that. Or recall that one of the greatest and oldest military tactics is to "divide and...conquer". Why does that work so well? Because when we are divided we are weakened. When we are on our own we may be strong, but we are not as strong as we are when we are united.

Our 13 colonies proved this over two centuries ago when they rose up as the United States of America. E pluribus Unum is the traditional motto of the United States. It means "out of many, one" in Latin. It refers to the colonies united into one nation symbolized by the great seal of the United States on the shield covering the eagle's breast which has 13 vertical stripes. The stripes represent the states all joined as one in solidarity which unites the whole. That gives me goose bumps when I think of and admire the brave, wise, visionary people who gave birth to our great nation.

At Spirit Ranch we had a high challenge ropes course complete with rock climbing, repelling, zip-lining, and other initiatives that rose 30 to 50 feet off the ground. When someone was up high they wore one or two harnesses that were attached to a belay rope. Belay is French for "attached or secured". These ropes had a 5,000 pound capacity and were in the able hands of trained, certified facilitators. So even if you didn't feel safe when you were so high off the ground, you really were safe.

At the conclusion of the day I would take a retired belay rope to illustrate how being united makes for strength (for safety we kept track of the number of uses or any damage and retired a rope and no longer used it for climbing). I would peel back the outer sheath and reveal 13 cords that had been woven together. Then I would take one of those cords and separate it into the 3 strings that made up each cord. 3 times 13 lets us know that there were 39 strings that had been "united" in this rope. I would then pull one of those strings out and begin to unravel it revealing countless spider web-size strands that were so small you could barely see them unless you held them up to the light.

Then I would hold the rope up dangling only from one of those tiny strands and ask, "when you were 50 feet above the ground today would you rather be belayed by this (the tiny strand) or this (the 5,000 lb. capacity rope). Of course the answer was obvious and I don't recall anyone actually voicing their reply.

The metaphor is we are simply one of those tiny strands. But we have great worth because if we intertwine ourselves with other tiny strands we create a string. And if those strings weave themselves together we have a cord. And if those cords are all contained in a sheath then we have a strong rope that will not be broken. This isn't news. Over 3,000 years ago Solomon wrote "two are better than one…a cord of three strands is not easily broken."

I do love the unity cornerstone. It stimulates:

- Encouragement
- Grace
- Compassion
- Strength

Write down what you did the last time you gave some one your encouragement.

Name some people who have been an encouragement to you in your life.

Have you received your gift of grace or are you too proud to do that? Why or why not?

Who needs grace from you right now? Who could benefit from you demonstrating such kindness?

Someone you know is suffering right now. Heartache, work challenges, family issues. Think how you can show your compassion for them.

Think of a story or two that illustrates the strength that unity has provided for you.

The seeds of joy can only be firmly planted in the pungent soil of the here and now while at the same time being tethered to eternity. Joy is fully rooted in the truth. Joy embraces all the senses and is fully awake to the laughter, the wonder, and the beauty present in the moment as well as the sorrow, the angst, and the fear. Joy says, "Even so, I have a reason to celebrate."

– Staci Eldredge

CHAPTER 8

THE CAPSTONE OF JOY

When a capstone is laid in place as the symbol of the completion of a magnificent structure there is celebration honoring the visionary architects and engineers, talented craftsmen, and skillful laborers. It is the opportunity to look back at what has been accomplished with joy and say, "There! It's finished!"

But, there's a difference for you when I talk about the joy capstone. When you and yours have successfully laid the four cornerstones you have every right to celebrate with joy what you are accomplishing. Notice I said accomplishing…not accomplished because the joy you experience should be recurring. It should not be a one-time accomplishment. There will be many days of joy as you revisit the four cornerstones, make corrections where needed, and employ all of their elements.

Perhaps now is the time to elaborate a bit on the word "joy". The more obvious and common synonyms are delight, bliss, or gladness. But there is a deeper meaning to the word, too, that is related to benefit or profit. As Staci Eldredge says on this chapter's cover page there is sorrow, angst, and fear. Yet, even in our struggles there is "benefit" as we mature and "profit" as we strengthen our character. Remember there is always *more* than what we see right now.

When you are in a place where people trust each other; where people agree upon and understand their expectations; where people get to exercise their freedom; and where people live and work together in unity there will be joy.

So what are the elements of the capstone? Let's start with *calm.* Chaos creates tension and stress. Order creates a feeling of, well, orderliness. Think about your closet at home. How do you feel when dirty clothes from the past two weeks are strewn all over the floor and the cleaning you picked up last week is still in the plastic bag hanging on a doorknob and you can't find the shoes you were planning to wear and then the light suddenly burns out and you're left standing in the dark? Would calm describe your emotions in that moment?

Now imagine that you've just spent an entire Saturday morning putting your closet back in order. The light is back on with a fresh bulb. The laundry has been done, folded, and put away. The clothes from the cleaners have been hung in order along with all your other pants, coats, and shirts. You've actually selected shoes to give away to charity and those you are keeping are on their shelves categorized by style and color. Now how are you feeling? Quite a difference isn't there?

In four cornerstone organizations and families there is a sense of calm. Life is still busy and even hectic at times. Deadlines still loom. Projects will still be challenging. People will still misbehave. But you are looking at all that through a lens of calm. It's like being in the eye of the storm…there is wind and rain all around you, but you remain calm.

One of the best examples of remaining calm is a story told by former president George W. Bush. We were hosting a fund raiser for a private school at Spirit Ranch and he was the guest speaker. It was a big event. A tent almost the size of a football field was set up in our meadow. In it were chandeliers hanging from the ceiling, tables beautifully set and decorated, a raised stage with two wingback chairs in a living room setting, and an audience of close to 1,500 guests. After a terrific meal was served the headmaster of the school and President Bush took their places in the two wingback chairs.

In this interview setting the headmaster asked excellent questions and the president gave excellent answers mixing in his humor and stories from his life in the White House. In the interview this question was asked; "What leadership quality would you share with us that helped you as president?" Without hesitation President Bush said "calm". And then he told his very personal version of that day of September 11, 2001...of being in the Florida classroom when his chief of staff, Andrew Card, told him that America was under attack. He remembered being flown about on Air Force One not being able to return to Washington until it was sure that the attack had ended. He recalled how difficult it was being apart from the First Lady and his daughters, his staff and his cabinet, his position of responsibility in the White House. But through it all he remained calm. Our daughter, Beth, has had a calm spirit since I first saw her in the delivery room. Growing up, whether on the tennis or basketball court, with her friends hanging out, or just being at home with two older brothers she was always just so emotionally level...never too high, never too low. As a wife, mother, business woman, and community volunteer she has maintained that same calm, orderly approach to living. And her household shows it...rarely chaotic, usually calm. She has such joy in her life and it's contagious!

Contentment is the next element of joy. There is an inner peace that is very difficult to put into words. It's the feeling that things are "ok" in spite of what may be going on in our lives. The Apostle Paul said, "I have learned to be content whatever the circumstances. I know what it is to be in need, and I know what it is to have plenty. I have learned the secret of being content in any and every situation, whether well fed or hungry, whether living in plenty or in want."[21]

Compare the house I lived in with Jayne Ann during the early days of our marriage to the one I live in today with Katherine. I bought a little cracker box house right after graduating from Texas Tech and that is where we lived when we got married. It had two tiny bedrooms with a tiny bathroom, a tiny kitchen, and a tiny living room all in 900 square feet. Two people could barely turn around in the bathroom. The one car garage held our used washer/dryer, lawnmower, and other "stuff" without any room for a car.

We made a breakfast table out of a piece of plywood and wrought iron legs and covered it with a table cloth. The entertainment center was one of those pressboard do-it-yourself things that held a small television and a stereo left over from high school. The living room was furnished with two used recliners and an old couch from her parents which we reupholstered in the gaudiest gold crushed velvet material you have ever seen. Guess what? We loved it. It was ours and we were completely content.

Now, almost five decades later, Katherine and I are grateful to live in a spacious, wonderful home. Incidentally, Katherine is a professional interior designer and trust me, we don't have any gold crushed velvet furniture in our house. Guess what? We love it and we are completely content.

See what I mean about being content regardless of circumstances? But read this carefully…I am not talking about being satisfied. There is a difference. You can be content but not be satisfied with your performance or your profits or your product because better is almost always possible. If I'm a major league pitcher and my earned run average is 3.97 I can live with that, but I know it can improve so I'm not satisfied. If I'm a concert pianist and I perform on stage in front of thousands and only strike one key wrong and nobody else but me notices, I may be content with the performance but I'm not yet satisfied.

Here's where I need to warn you about lack of satisfaction. Don't let it turn into perfectionism or expecting outcomes that may truly be unreachable. This is coming from me, a recovering perfectionist. Our son, Matt, who was a major league pitcher, now gives private pitching lessons in an indoor workout facility. One day he was telling me about a very positive step that he had taken in making his business more successful. I told him that was great! And then with the best of intentions, I said, "And if you would do such and such it would be even better!" He looked me in the eye and said, "You know, Dad, nothing's ever quite good enough for you, is it?"

His words broke my heart. I didn't feel sorry for myself. Instead, I hated that I had taken the air out of his sail by making my comment. Then I wondered if I had put too much pressure on all three of our children all of their lives. The point I'm trying to make is this. Don't settle for mediocrity. Better is possible. But don't take that too far either. Sometimes contentment means accepting that "good" really is "good enough."

Confidence is the next element of joy. How could it not be? People trust you and vice versa. You have clear and confirmed understanding of you mission, project task, assignment or whatever. You are free to create and have fun. Your confidence level goes up and up in a four cornerstone organization.

Our son Tim is a practicing physician. Not bragging, but he is respected in his specialty and is in demand not only as a doctor, but as a business leader and speaker as well. I remember so well when he would share his experiences when he was in medical school and was rounding with several specialties. From pediatrics to cardiology to psychology (and others) he would shake his head and wonder if we would ever be able to learn enough to be effective with his patients. That has certainly changed. Now, not only is he competent he has just the right blend of humility and confidence. I think that is attributable to the joy he has in serving his patients and his community.

The last element I will describe is that of *completion*. Being complete doesn't mean the same thing as being finished. Being complete means wholeness...having all the needed parts. When a car rolls off the assembly line it has been completed. But its journey is only just beginning. When meal preparation is complete it isn't yet finished. Instead it is ready for enjoyment.

In the movie *Jerry Maguire*, there's a romantic moment when, playing the title character, Tom Cruise walks into the living room of his on-again, off-again girlfriend Dorothy Boyd played by Renee Zellweger. They have had some struggles in their relationship but he realizes that he loves her and wants to be with her. So during his impassioned plea to her he says, "You...complete...me." And he tries to go on and say more, but she says, "Shut up. You had me at hello." Now guys if you don't remember that scene I can assure you your special girl does! The lesson in those lines is this: being complete doesn't mean being finished.

It means you're whole. And isn't it interesting that takes us right back to where we started with being wholehearted.

Do you experience this kind of joy where you work and live? If not, why not? Which element(s) of which cornerstone is missing or being neglected or could be improved upon. The truths contained in the cornerstones are universal and ageless so there is no way I could possibly take credit for any of them. I am glad that I've been able to distill these concepts and put them in some sort of logical order. But, that being said, my greatest pride (and it's the good kind of pride as opposed to arrogance) is that I haven't been able to find any situation or problem or opportunity that in one way or another can't be addressed with these cornerstones. Think for a minute. What challenge are you facing right now? Look back over these pages and see if something doesn't jump out at you that says, "Here! What you need is right here!"

When people look to you for leadership do they see a person who is calm? I hope so. Leaders who are turbulent, agitated, nervous or ruffled tend to reflect those tendencies on others. Which are you?

Think of some leaders you've worked with. On a scale of 1-10 with 1 being turbulent and 10 being calm, how would you rank them? Which did you enjoy working for more?

Write down a few words about contentment. Where are you right now at home or at work? Are you at peace? If so, how do you share that? If not, what's your next step to finding a remedy?

Is there something that you're not satisfied with even though you may be experiencing contentment? What is that something and how can you go to work on improving it?

One of the best explanations I've heard about the word humility is this. Don't shrink from the glory of who you were created to be; shrink in the shadow of the One who created you. In other words, be confident without being arrogant. Describe where you are with your confidence.

Write down three things you will do within the next 7 days to build up someone else's confidence.

Treat yourself to some examples of feeling complete or of a major accomplishment that was completed. How can you capture that feeling again?

Do not despise these small beginnings for the Lord rejoices to see the work begin.

– Zechariah

CHAPTER 9

NOW WHAT?

This book is relatively short for a couple of reasons. One, there is only some much truth to go around. People write and speak about the same basic concepts in many different ways using a variety of great examples. I wanted to just get down to the "blocking and tackling" basics of leadership. Hopefully, the four cornerstones and the capstone gives you those basics in language that is easy to understand.

The other reason is that I'd rather you put the principles to work rather than continuing reading and reading. It doesn't matter what you read or hear about leadership. What matters is what you do with it. So this is what I suggest you do. Follow the teaching method of "watch one, do one, teach one."

I'll give you an example. Our daughter Summer (Katherine's daughter, but I claim her as mine too), was the 4th person hired in her company shortly after it was started. The company is an internet based retailer of quality handmade boots that recently, in addition, has opened bricks and mortar retail locations.[22] When Summer started in their customer experience department (a department of one at that time), she didn't know about the products or the industry. So she observed and took notes and studied and asked a ton of questions. And, my guess is that she made her share of mistakes along the way. But she was *watching*.

Then she got the hang of it and before too long was processing hundreds and hundreds of orders for boots. In other words she was *doing*. Now she has dozens of people working for her as the vice president of customer experience and she is *teaching* them what she has learned.

What you have read about this far would be considered "watching" (or discovering according to the understanding cornerstone). Now take the next step of "doing" by using the worksheets in the appendices.

If you do nothing with them then that's your decision. But just realize that the laws of the harvest will never be broken. Do you know what those laws are? Well, here they are.

Harvest Law #1 – You always harvest what you plant. If you plant apple seeds you don't get oranges or grapes. You get apples. In similar fashion if you plant good effort you will get a good harvest. If you don't plant at all then there will be no harvest.

Harvest Law #2 – You never harvest in the same season you plant in. You always have to wait. On the South Plains of West Texas we plant cotton…lots of cotton. The seeds are usually planted in May. After months of water, fertilizer, weed and insect control, the harvest (known as stripping) takes place in October and November. When you begin practicing the cornerstone elements you may not see the results you want right away, but they will eventually happen.

Harvest Law #3 – You harvest more than you plant. In other words the old saying "you get out of something what you put into it" isn't exactly accurate. The fact is, you get *more* out of what you put into something. Consider the apple tree. The average apple tree produces about 300 apples in a growing season. Let's say that the average apple contains 5 apple seeds. So all things being equal, one apple tree will produce about 1,500 seeds per season. Those 1,500 seeds will then potentially produce 450,000 apples, and another 2,250,000 seeds.[23]

So here is my challenge to you. Begin. Anywhere. But just begin. Perhaps you will use only one of the worksheets in the appendices to start with. That will help you move into the "doing" phase. Then when you feel like you know enough to share with someone else on that particular idea you should be ready to "teach" that person or group of persons. It is only when we teach (mentor/coach) others that we have truly learned something ourselves.

Good luck. No, never mind good luck. Instead, good work! That is what it will take to become a four cornerstone and capstone leader.

Art... not science... is what it takes to lead. You can manage with science (data, methods, policies, schedules). But you have to lead with an artist's hand.

– David A. Miller

WEEKLY WISDOM

There are, indeed, techniques and mechanisms that we employ as leaders. I've written about some of them on the preceding pages. Yet, while we manage projects and tasks and budgets, we must realize that we *lead* people. Leading is accomplished (or not) 100% through relationships (or the lack of them). Influencing others to follow you is successful only if there is mutual respect and knowledge about one another.

Oh sure, another person can be motivated on a short term basis with fear, dictatorial intimidation, unfeeling and uncaring communication. Yes, "being the boss" can work. But, long-term there is something much better.

And that "better" is leading people *wisely*. I've found the best sources of wisdom are these:

- Listening to other admirable people and putting their experiences to work for me
- Learning from my own experiences, both painful and joyful
- Reading and applying scriptural truth

So on the next 104 pages, I will tell you some stories (my experiences), quote some wise people from history (time-tested wisdom), and give you scripture references from the Bible that, when applied, can change lives.

You will see that I've given you plenty of room for you to write your thoughts. May I encourage you (have the courage) to take some time each week and think; ponder; meditate; and record your thoughts. There are nuggets of wisdom more valuable than gold if you take the time to look for them.

And, as you read, like Billy Graham used to say, "May the Lord bless you real good."

WEEK 1
CLOUDY, LET ME INTRODUCE YOU TO CLARITY

Do you accept the premise that without clarity, you experience some leadership challenges due to cloudiness? Things sure seem cloudy to me sometimes. But if you and I are clear on where we want to lead our teams, then we can enjoy the benefit of *transparency*. And being transparent allows others to follow your direction...see your heart...be captured by the clarity of your vision.

But once again, how do we get that clarity? First, you and I both know that you don't just "get it" and "keep it". Having clarity (and the certainty and confidence and competence that goes with it) is an ongoing, never-ending proposition of *really* listening. But, that's ok. So is *really* bathing and *really* eating and *really* sleeping and *really* breathing. We keep doing those things because we need or want to, right?

In the next few weeks, I'm going to be sharing something I discovered in a mountain cabin hideaway a couple of months after my wife, Jayne Ann, died. It's related to hearing "the call" which leads to clarity which leads to...well, you get the picture. I call the discovery "The Five S's".

For now we see in a mirror dimly, but then face to face. Now I know in part; then I shall know fully, even as I have been fully known. ***– 1 Corinthians 13:12*** (NASB)

ACTION ITEM

What subjects do you need clarity on? Think hard and list them on the opposite page.

WEEK 1 – NOTES

WEEK 2
SANCTUARY

A sanctuary, in its original meaning, is a sacred place. By extension a sanctuary is a safe haven...a hideaway...a place of safe retreat.

For me, unless I am in such a place, it's difficult to listen to that inner voice that calls to me. Such a place could be in the privacy of my home office...or in my truck as I'm parked near a field of bluebonnets...or in the shower as the steaming hot water cascades over my shoulders...or in a bamboo hut in the rain forest of Costa Rica...or in the secluded mountain cabin where I invested several days in listening.

It was in that little New Mexico cabin (see photo) that I was in the 3rd month of grieving the loss of my wife of 40+ years. But, it was also there that I was seeing the world through fresh eyes. That inner voice (don't *you* hear that voice sometimes, too?) was guiding me, giving me *clarity* because I was taking the time to listen.

I would not have heard the calling during those few days if I had been at work or in a noisy restaurant or at a grandchild's game or with the TV blaring the latest news or sports or whatever. I know that I needed to be hidden away...in a safe haven...in a sanctuary. So, step one in really listening...find yourself a sanctuary. It may be as close as your closet or backyard.

Let them construct a sanctuary for Me,
that I may dwell among them. – Exodus 25:8 (NASB)

ACTION ITEM

Where will your sanctuary be?

WEEK 2 – NOTES

WEEK 3
SOLITUDE

Short-term solitude can be valued as a time when you may work, think or rest without being disturbed. It is desirable for the sake of privacy. Once you are in your sanctuary, you really need to be alone. Not lonely, I hope, but in a private place. While we were built for being with others (together has power), we none-the-less need time by ourselves, as well.

Sure, thing David. I'll just lock my 3 kids in the closet with some bread and water; or I'll just excuse myself from the classroom and let the students learn themselves; or I'll simply walk away from the 10 appointments I have scheduled for today...all so I can be alone. Get real.

Well, please forgive me. But YOU get real. Sooner or later you are going to have to find a place (your place of refuge) and get alone and *breathe*. Find ten minutes or an hour and sneak away. Better yet, schedule a weekend or a week and get some help with those kids and appointments, etc. You'll be glad you did. It's a lot easier to listen when the door is closed...and locked.

Now in the morning, having risen a long while before daylight, He went out and departed to a solitary place. – Mark 1:35 (NKJV)

ACTION ITEM

Put some alone time on your calendar. It may be daily, but brief. Or it may be a full retreat.

WEEK 3 – NOTES

WEEK 4
SABBATICAL

The main Bible passage for the concept of a sabbatical is found in Genesis, in which God rested (literally, "ceased" from his labor) after creating the universe. It is applied to people (Jew and Gentile, slave and free) and even to beasts of burden in one of the Ten Commandments (Exodus 20:8-11). All agriculture was stopped during these periods, so even the land itself was given a Sabbath.

Are you kidding? Even the land was given a rest? I've been told to "give it a rest", but I think they were really just telling me to shut up. Well, that's kinda what this whole thing about "sabbatical" is about. At least that's the next step in being able to listen internally.

For now, don't think as a sabbatical as taking a month or year or some other time off from work to write a book or complete a research project or travel around the world. Those may be good activities, but that's the point…they are *activities*…as in action. Once you are in your sanctuary and you are alone in solitude, then simply…stop. S-T-O-P. Cease. Quit.

Yes. Just cease what you are doing.

Above is one of the incredible views on my sabbatical from my bamboo hut in the jungle of Costa Rica. Do you think I would have ever seen it or dozens of other sights or heard the macaws or howler monkeys or surf crashing on the rocks 50 yards from the hut if I hadn't have stopped being Mr. CEO for a few days???? Nope.

Cease striving and know that I am God. - Psalm 46:10 (NASB)

ACTION ITEM

What are you going to stop doing? And when?

WEEK 4 – NOTES

WEEK 5
STILLNESS

All of these "S's" are hard. This one is hard, too. I know. But I got to wondering as I discovered the Five S's that if the reason they are so powerful, especially if used in combination, is because they are indeed difficult to practice. I think that may especially be true for people with leadership responsibilities.

But then, I also thought about the adage "anything worth having is worth working for". Well, putting all these S's in practice may be work, but this one…stillness…means we are NOT working. In fact, it's the absence of work for a while.

Author Martha Beck[24] says that doing nothing is the most productive activity you will ever undertake. By doing nothing she means literally *doing nothing.* Not problem solving. Not planning. Not even prayer. Doing nothing is being still, quieting your mind and just being.

This is so hard in our social media world. All kinds of noise, both audible and visual, crowd into our minds leaving us exhausted.

Now, be still. Just for a little while…be com – plete – ly still.

The Lord will fight for you; you need only to be still.
– Exodus 14:14 (NIV)

ACTION ITEM

Shut everything out. Turn off your mind. Close your eyes. Think of nothing. Be STILL.

WEEK 5 - NOTES

WEEK 6
SILENCE

The final "S" is Silence. As I write that word I long for more of it.

Here are some words from Rob Bell's video, Noise.

"Why is silence so hard to deal with? Why is it so much easier for us to live our lives with a lot of things going on all the time than to just be in silence? We're constantly surrounded with "voices" that are influencing us on how to think, feel, and behave. Movies, music, TV, internet, cell phones, and a never-ending barrage of advertising. There's always something going on. Always noise in our lives. But maybe there's a connection between the amount of noise in our lives and our inability to hear God. If God sometimes feels distant to us, maybe it's not because he's not talking to us, but simply because we aren't really listening."

Hhhmmm. Sound familiar? Perhaps hitting a little too close to home for comfort? Boy, it sure does for me. Especially, since I like to hear myself talk too much. (If you know me, you don't have to be quite so quick to agree!).

But, I will tell you this. When this last piece of the Five-S puzzle falls into place, then you have a transformational experience that is unforgettable. It is both amazing and sometimes scary to see what life has brought to me and for me when I have (1) retreated to a sanctuary; (2) found solitude; (3) taken a sabbatical; (4) sat in stillness; and (5) practiced silence. Oh my!

There is a time for everything and a season for every activity under the heavens: a time to be silent and a time to speak... – Ecclesiastes 3:1, 7b (NIV)

ACTION ITEM

Don't speak. Turn off all media. Shut down your phones. Turn off your computer. Practice silence.

WEEK 6 – NOTES

WEEK 7
SOME PEOPLE ARE WORTH MELTING FOR

Years ago I went to see the Disney movie "Frozen" not once, but twice (different cities, different grandkids). In the Disney tradition it is a great movie with princesses, heroes, and villains.

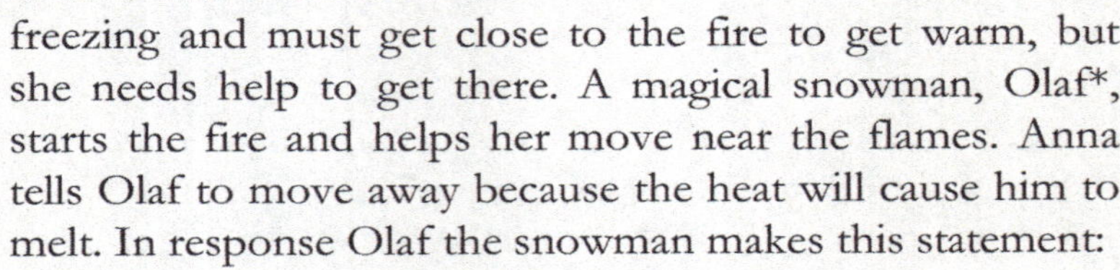

There is one scene in the movie in which Princess Anna* is near freezing and must get close to the fire to get warm, but she needs help to get there. A magical snowman, Olaf*, starts the fire and helps her move near the flames. Anna tells Olaf to move away because the heat will cause him to melt. In response Olaf the snowman makes this statement:

"Some people are worth melting for"…..

As I thought about that line I could not help but think how many people have "melted" for me and our family over the years. I will always be grateful to them for that. Perhaps if we all would "melt" for others…even if they weren't "worth melting for"… we could make a difference.

You know this concept isn't new…..Jesus said it this way, "No greater love has any person than to give their very own life for someone else". And then He did.

*Frozen, Princess Anna and Olaf are registered by The Disney Corporation.

One who has unreliable friends soon comes to ruin, but there is a friend who sticks closer than a brother. – Proverbs 18:24 (NIV)

ACTION ITEM

List the people who have "melted" for you. Now write them a thank you note or give them a call.

WEEK 7 - NOTES

WEEK 8
FREEDOM FROM FEAR

I'm discovering how many of us are motivated or better said "de-motivated" by fear. The fear of failure; the fear of the unknown; the fear of looking dumb; the fear of not being accepted; the fear of not measuring up; the fear of not having what it takes; or the fear of "whatever". Fear seems to almost paralyze us and if it doesn't then it certainly causes us to hesitate…to doubt…to put off some things we either really want to do (like follow our passion or dream).

Not too long ago a group of outstanding college students was at Spirit Ranch for a day of leadership development. The day had a positive impact on all of them, some more than others. I had three students come up to me afterward who not only hugged me, they held me, seemingly not wanting to let go. Each of them, through their tears of gratitude, told me that we had helped them overcome some lifelong fears through their experiences that day. They felt released…set free…to follow their dreams. Wow!

When Jesus started his ministry he restated Isaiah 61:1-2 (NIV) which, in part, says "He (God) has sent me to bind up the brokenhearted, to proclaim freedom for the captives, and release from darkness for the prisoners". So, how about the rest of us? Shouldn't we feel released…freed, as well? Let's put fear aside and go for it as leaders, spouses, parents, friends, as people who have been set free.

There is no fear in love; but perfect love casts out fear.
– 1 John 4:18 (NASB)

ACTION ITEM

Name your fear(s). Now release them and they will release you.

WEEK 8 – NOTES

WEEK 9
OUR INHERITENCE

The old phrase, "to have one's ears pinned back", serves as a window into a horse's mental state. Normally, a horse will hold its ears erect and alert. But when frightened or angry, the horse will put its ears back against its head. It's best to pay attention to this overt signal!

Like the horse in the pic, every horse has been known to lay those ears back flat from time to time. And, perhaps with good reason.

Hhhmmm….sounds like some people you know, doesn't it? When even the least bit threatened (ego, status, security, position) some folks "pin their ears back". Others, just let things roll of their backs and keep moving, often with grace and laughter and class. Why is that?

Inheritance, that's why. Somewhere back there, we inherited a sense of fear or anger or submission or lack of self-worth. Or we may have inherited confidence and value and love and encouragement. We certainly all have had at least a portion of all those at one time or another, right? The people you are leading, regardless of what setting you find yourself in, have inherited these things, too. Some will cause negative reactions because of their history. Learn what those trigger points are and lead accordingly. How? Try Paul's suggestion of "speaking the truth in love". And when that doesn't work…do it again. And when that fails…do it again. And when you get tired of doing it…do it again. The ears will eventually come forward again.

Anxiety weighs down the heart, but a kind word cheers it up.
– Proverbs 12:25 (NIV)

ACTION ITEM

Who do you need to lovingly speak truth into?
When will you do it? What words will you use?

WEEK 9 – NOTES

WEEK 10
THERE IS ALWAYS MORE TO THE PICTURE

How many faces do you see in this picture? Can you tell who might be angry? Happy? How many are sad? Is it cold? What is that laying on the ground to the side of the tree? Is the tree dead or simply dormant?

I can't answer all of those questions with absolute certainty. I have some immediate guesses...can draw some initial conclusions. But until I get to *know* more about this scene, I simply can't be sure.

I count 11 faces. How many do you get?

Same with people. How dare we assume so much about others when we haven't even made an attempt to get to know them?!?! Remember there may be more than what we can see. (By the way, did you count the baby?)

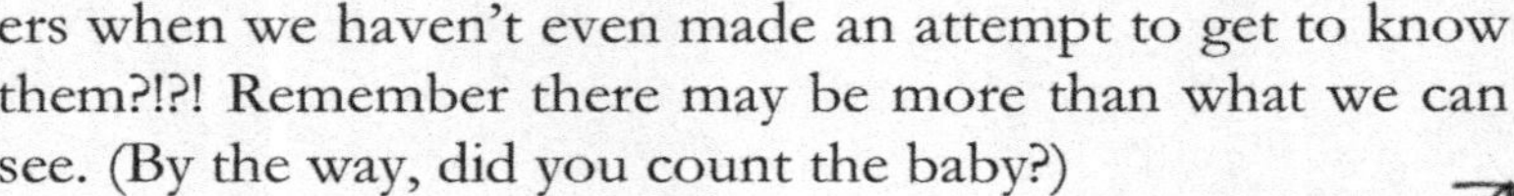

The heart of the discerning acquires knowledge, for the ears of the wise seek it out. – Proverbs 18:15 (NIV)

ACTION ITEM

List people or situations you have misjudged using your first perception. Now learn from your list.

WEEK 10 - NOTES

WEEK 11
THE FREEDOM OF INNOCENCE

For me it was on "Blue Baby". For the cowboy in this picture it's on his horse. Where was it for you? In the sandbox? Reading under the covers at night with a flashlight after bedtime? Swinging on the monkey bars in the park? Falling asleep on the floor by your dog? Having your mom tickle your face as it lay in her lap? Flying high above the head of your dad as he twirled you around?

Go back to that age of innocence for you...just for a while. Even if you have some really bad memories from "those days", think of that one place you were safe...there was pure joy...there was the freedom of being innocent. Now, live that way again. Come on...try it. Just for a while.

Blue Baby? My incredible bike that as a 6-year old allowed me to ride like the wind. I'm smiling...

I will maintain my innocence and never let go of it...
– Job 27:6a (NIV)

ACTION ITEM

Go down memory lane and get back some joy from those innocent times in your life. See if you can recreate them for yourself and for others.

WEEK 11 – NOTES

WEEK 12
EXPRESS YOURSELF...EVEN IF IT'S MESSY

Ok, you can *impress* someone (sometimes good, sometimes not, but always only one chance for that first impression). You can *suppress* subjects in your mind (I have no clue how that works...I just know we do it). You can *compress* your clothes as you jam them into your suitcase so you don't have to check it on the airplane. Dictators *oppress* their subjects. (I would never accuse you as a leader of doing such a thing, of course). OK, I'm about to stop before I *depress* you.

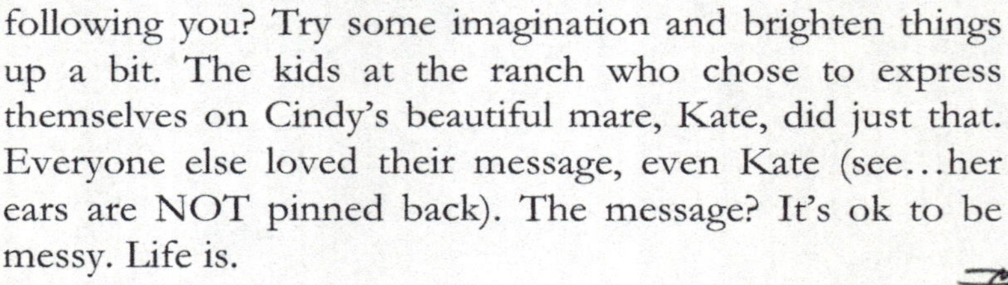

How about the way we ***express*** ourselves? How do we let the world know how we think and feel? How do you express yourself to those who are following you? Try some imagination and brighten things up a bit. The kids at the ranch who chose to express themselves on Cindy's beautiful mare, Kate, did just that. Everyone else loved their message, even Kate (see...her ears are NOT pinned back). The message? It's ok to be messy. Life is.

My mouth will speak words of wisdom; the meditation of my heart will give you understanding. – Psalm 49:3 (NIV)

ACTION ITEM

Examine the way you express your thoughts and feelings. List some ways you could liven things up a bit to increase understanding and fun.

WEEK 12 – NOTES

WEEK 13
CONTROL

People confide in me regarding both personal and professional problems (aka, challenges, issues, opportunities). And I find myself wanting to "fix" those problems so I take charge and begin prescribing the perfect solution by saying "this is what you ought to do". Why? Because I really do want to help solve the problem! Right? Maybe. But, what most people really want is for someone to simply listen and try to understand.

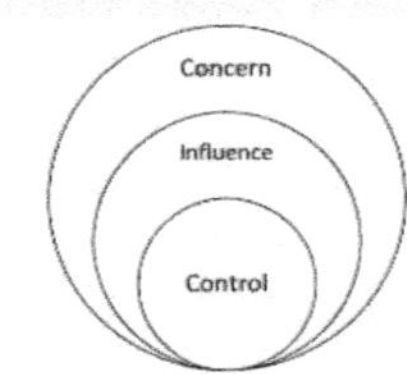

There *are* many things you and I can control; choices that we make every day to get out of bed, brush our teeth and hair, go to work, encourage the kids, volunteer for the club, etc. But there is *so* much that we can't control; our next heartbeat or breath, the other guy running the red light, the cancer cells, the tears of a clown…you get the picture.

Consider the three circles above and decide what you can't control, but can influence or have concern about. Then let go of those things and focus on what you can control.

I've said it before; I'll say it again: I have to let go. Let go…of those things that I can't or don't need to control. Maybe you should, too?

Who of you by worrying can add a single hour to your life? Since you cannot do this very little thing, why do you worry about the rest? – Luke 12:25-26 (NIV)

ACTION ITEM

Make a list of things you need to let go of and those you need to hold on to. See how you can simplify your life by doing so.

WEEK 13 – NOTES

WEEK 14
FATIGUE - FOG - FLIRTATION

My friend and renowned leadership speaker/author, Dr. Ken Jones, shared the thoughts below with our board of directors a few years ago. I know he has presented it to many others, as well. It's my privilege to pass his thoughts along to you using my paraphrased version.

Fatigue, be it mental, physical, emotional, or spiritual, is not only unpleasant; it can also be dangerous. Driving when you're too tired; discussing a sensitive issue when you're emotionally raw; making a decision when your brain is worn to a frazzle. Yet, fatigue is going to happen to all of us in one way or another from time to time.

As Ken says, when we get fatigued, we find ourselves in a *fog*...a fog of indecision or deceleration or paralysis. Think of what it's like to try to drive on the highway through the fog. It's risky.

And being in a fog leads to *flirtation*. We tend to start thinking about things we wouldn't normally think about. We flirt with something like trading in excellence for mediocrity. Like escaping into fantasies. Like having an affair. Like quitting on a job or a team or a family or a friend. Such flirtation can ultimately be disastrous. Don't flirt. Get some rest instead.

Even youths grow tired and weary, and young men stumble and fall; but those who hope in the Lord will renew their strength. They will soar on wings like eagles; they will run and not grow weary, they will walk and not be faint. - Isaiah 40:31 (NIV)

ACTION ITEM

List the symptoms of your fatigue. Make a conscious decision to get out of the fog. And, if you need to read next week's wisdom about rest right now please go ahead.

WEEK 14 - NOTES

WEEK 15
REST

Late one Friday afternoon I was visiting with some of my friends who told me how tired they felt as the week ended. Earlier in the day I had facilitated an outstanding group of leaders of a financial institution and they relayed to me how often they feel overextended in their job responsibilities. And, as my day draws to a close I find myself pretty worn out, too.

Fatigue-Fog-Flirtation. How do we deal with this pattern that is all too common? There is only one antidote that I know of that works. And it is like bathing or eating...you have to do it over and over.

The antidote is *rest.* If you're physically worn out, get some extra sleep this weekend. If you're emotionally tired, seek a trusted friend to "unload" some of that baggage. If you're mentally exhausted, please turn off your mental motor for a while... if you don't it will overheat. And if you're spiritually dehydrated, take a drink of the grace that is available to us all from our Creator. And remember, even He took the 7th day off from work.

Rest well this week. Rest well.

Come to me, all you who are weary and burdened, and I will give you rest. – Matthew 11:28 (NIV)

ACTION ITEM

Plan some time for rest. Make sure you're getting 7-8 hours of sleep. Find a friend who will listen to you without judgment or advice. Turn off the TV. Put down your phone. And don't forget to pray.

WEEK 15 – NOTES

WEEK 16
BEAUTY

Beauty may be the most powerful force on earth in driving our leadership decisions. Of course we know there are budgets and strategies and market conditions and stockholder demands and all that "stuff".

Yet, often we find ourselves inspired by the splendor and majesty of a sunset whether it is high in the Colorado Rockies, rapidly sinking into the Pacific Ocean, or disappearing beneath the west Texas horizon. I find myself intrigued and inspired by the priceless innocence of young children. The flowers in Butchart Gardens take my breath away.

Why would we even think about concerning ourselves as leaders with the beauty around us?

Because beauty is the antidote for pain. And there is so much pain in our lives: depression, divorce, bankruptcy, cancer, heart issues of every kind, betrayal, and loss…loss of a job; a friend; an opportunity; a beloved.

Where do we turn to? I turn to beauty. Those soft blue eyes and wispy hair and disarming smile of my daughter pictured above takes me away from all my cares. Her beauty also resides in her heart, her voice, and her hugs. I've given her a rose for each year of her life starting with her 16th birthday. I think she is more beautiful than the roses. Look at your children and remember beautiful memories with them.

Let beauty work for you as a leader.

He has made everything beautiful in its time. He has also set eternity in the human heart… – Ecclesiastes 3:11 (NIV)

ACTION ITEM

Reflect upon things of beauty in your life.
Let them relieve pain in your life and in others.

WEEK 16 - NOTES

WEEK 17
IDEAS CAN BE PAINFUL

I'll bet you can think of more than one instance when you felt pain because an idea that you strongly believed in was shot down. I've been there too, believe me. And yet I am here to encourage you NOT to suppress your ideas. Yes, fear of embarrassment or rejection really does stifle us sometimes from sharing our creative thoughts.

So let's agree on this...there are no bad ideas, just ideas whose time may not have yet come.

The idea of a wrist telephone? The idea of Uber? The idea of a microwave oven? The idea of a talking gecko? The idea of a horseless carriage? The idea of sticky note? All of these must have seemed "crazy" at one point in time. And yet, we experience them every day.

Well, we may have to modify some of our ideas, yet I hope you will never stop imagining and sharing your ideas...good or not so good. Only time will tell.

Fix your thoughts on what is true, and honorable, and right, and pure, and lovely, and admirable. Think about things that are excellent and worthy of praise. – Philippians 4:8 (NLT)

ACTION ITEM

Have any ideas you want to share? Write them on the opposite page and make plans to tell others of them. Don't have any ideas to share? Then get busy creating some.

WEEK 17 - NOTES

WEEK 18
A FIRM GRIP AND A SMILE

On February 11, 2000 I slept in for just a few extra minutes. Overslept, actually. By the time I arrived at the hospital Dad had already been wheeled into surgery for his heart by-pass procedure so I didn't get to say "see you later". Less than two hours later an O.R. nurse came into the waiting room where my family was calmly chatting. She said the surgeon had "run into problems". Our "chat" quickly turned into fervent prayers. Late that afternoon (those few hours seemed to equate to an eternity) we were told that they had done all they could do. A few minutes later I was gripping the now lifeless hand that used to shake mine with firmness and a smile...always a smile.

I felt like a small child again that day even though I was a half-century old. I feel that way again today as I write this. No wonder I cherish this photo of me next to him as...a little child.

Still missing you, pal. Anticipating a great reunion someday. Until then, I hope to honor you with my life... and a firm grip and a smile for others.

The father of a righteous child has great joy; a man who fathers a wise son rejoices in him. ***– Proverbs 23:24*** (NIV)

ACTION ITEM

This week's action item is simple. Give all you meet a firm handshake and a smile. You will change their day when you do... maybe even their life. Write their names so you won't forget.

WEEK 18 – NOTES

WEEK 19
TRUE NORTH

True north (geodetic north) is the direction along the earth's surface towards the geographic North Pole. True geodetic north usually differs from magnetic north (the direction a compass points toward the magnetic north pole), and from grid north (the direction northwards along the grid lines of a map projection).

The direction of astronomical true north is marked in the skies by the north celestial pole. This is within about 1 degree of the position of Polaris, so that the star appears to trace a tiny circle in the sky each day. Due to the precession of the Earth's axis, true north rotates in an arc with respect to the stars that takes approximately 25,000 years to complete. In 2012 Polaris made its closest approach to the celestial North Pole.

I don't think I understand any of that! But I do know what true north has to do with leadership. Everything. If you don't know what your "true north" is...your vision, mission, goals, guiding principles...then how do you expect anyone to follow you?

Where are you headed? That is where you are going unless you decide to get and stay TRUE to yourself and head in the direction of your true north.

Trust in the Lord with all your heart and lean not on your own understanding; in all your ways submit to him and he will make your paths straight. – Proverbs 3:5-6 (NIV)

ACTION ITEM

Refer to the appendix related to your purpose, mission, vision, and values statements. Make sure you are headed true north by creating and living by these statements.

WEEK 19 - NOTES

WEEK 20
THE WOUNDS OF OUR LIVES

In his dissertation, *True Self, False Self* Richard Rohr says: "'The word 'innocent' from its Latin root means 'not wounded'. That's how we all start life. We're all innocent. It doesn't have anything to do with moral right or wrong. It has to do with not being wounded yet. We start unwounded. We start innocent, but the killing of our holy innocence by power and abuse (as in the killing of the Holy Innocents by Herod [Matthew 2:1-23]) is an archetypal image of what eventually happens to all of us. Probably it has to happen for us to grow up.

We can't stay unwounded. We have to leave the garden, so to speak. It is this movement out and back between the loneliness and desperation of the false self and the fullness of the True Self that is the process of transformation. That's how we move to consciousness and inner freedom."

Leaders (meaning moms, dads, CEO's, pilots, pastors, administrators, partners...in other words *all of us*...) are wounded. We are no longer "innocent" and there is pain in that. But leaders also are overcomers. Leaders also get up off the ground. Leaders also endure the pain, wipe the blood off, grieve the loss and then move on to fight again... to win again...to *lead* again.

You can do it. Come on...get up...let's get back in the battle. The victory *is* ahead.

He heals the brokenhearted and binds up their wounds.
– Psalm 147:3 (NIV)

ACTION ITEM

You've been wounded. Take time to heal. Keep in mind others are hurting, too. What can you do to (1) help yourself achieve victory and (2) help someone else achieve theirs?

WEEK 20 – NOTES

WEEK 21
WHY?

Why was the lovely freshman coed taken in an automobile accident at the age of 19?

Why are we fortunate to have so many friends and loved ones? Or…why *don't* we have many?

Why, when in his prime, did the pastor succumb to cancer? He was only 58 years old.

Why do some live to be 100+ with little or few health problems?

Why did Jennifer have a brain tumor at age 6?

Why am I fortunate enough to be able to type this instead of having limp, paralyzed hands hanging at my side? And why do you have the sight to read it?

Please…as much as we crave (perhaps even demand) answers to these "why" questions…may I kindly suggest that there simply aren't any adequate earthly answers. I wish there were, but wishing or worrying won't produce the answers for us. Believe me, I've tried.

The unanswerable seems to be a connector for us. So in the absence of the answers, cling to your faith; hold tightly to your friends; cherish your family members; love and respect yourself. What more can we do?

For my thoughts are not your thoughts neither are your ways my ways, declares the Lord. As the heavens are higher than the earth, so are my ways higher than your ways and my thoughts than your thoughts. – Isaiah 55:8-9 (NIV)

ACTION ITEM

List as many blessings in your life as possible on the opposite page. Then be grateful for them. Doing so won't make your life challenges go away, but it will help your perspective and mindset.

WEEK 21 - NOTES

WEEK 22
SEND FLOWERS

I didn't have the privilege of knowing Mr. Jamison. Yet, I like him though never having had the opportunity to meet him. He came to me via his obituary in the newspaper one morning. His age isn't stated, but since he was a member of the Fighting Aggie Class of '61, I would guess him to be about 75 or so when he passed away. He was married to his wife for 54 years and had 4 children and 2 granddaughters, all of whom apparently adored him.

Why pay a tribute to Mr. Jamison here? Simply because of what the family requested in lieu of flowers. They asked, instead, for you to "send them (the flowers) to one you love or make a small gesture of kindness to someone who needs it." Wow! What an unselfish gesture!

"*Someone who needs it.*" Hhhmmm...now who could that be? How about the very next person you come in contact with. And the person after that. And the person after that. After all, we *all* need small gestures of kindness. Maybe a few flowers too.

Be kind and compassionate to one another, forgiving each other, just as in Christ God forgave you. – Ephesians 4:32 (NIV)

ACTION ITEM

Think of people to whom you could give a kind gesture. Flowers? Maybe. Or maybe something else. But, as the Nike ad says, "just do it".

WEEK 22 - NOTES

WEEK 23
A CALLING

There were 12 of us that ran around together in high school. We hung out mostly on ball fields and in gymnasiums and, on Friday nights, Bob's Café. Mrs. Bob's pies were the best in America. Fifty plus years later almost all of us still go on an annual retreat to the lake or the mountains.

I have to share with you two events, both of which happened on January 4, 2014, that in their own way illustrate how different people are called in different ways by different voices with much different outcomes.

That day would have been Jim's 65th birthday. He was one of my closest friends since 7th grade. The voice (voices?) that were the loudest to Jim convinced him that life on this earth was no longer for him. So, he followed the call to end his. I have no answers for this...only tears as I see him standing in this photograph of "the gang" that is in my office.

That same day was also Stan's wedding day! (He's also in the picture.) Stan lost his wife a decade ago to ALS, a cruel disease. But on 1/4/14 he "answered the call" to take a new bride and enter an exciting new era in his life. He and Jane are enjoying life to the fullest.

Do you recognize that we need to *ignore* some voices? And other voices call us into new adventure and opportunity? We are all being called. So, whose voice are you listening to?

God's voice thunders in marvelous ways; he does great things beyond our understanding. – Job 37:5 (NIV)

ACTION ITEM

Listen carefully. What inner voice are you hearing? Write its message on the opposite page. Seek help if you need it. Share this thought with a safe person.

WEEK 23 - NOTES

WEEK 24
HYPERCRITICAL IS RELATED TO HYPOCRITICAL

A long time ago my favorite leader advised people to "get the plank out of their own eyes before trying to remove the splinter in another's". I need to remind myself of this truth over and over.

I take much too much pride (aka self-centeredness) in "suggesting" to others or "observing" in others how they could do things better. Better? What if their way is simply different…not necessarily better?

But, aren't my intentions good? Don't I simply want the other person to benefit from my perspective? Looking at myself in the proverbial mirror…probably not. I most likely just want to score another "win" in the hypercritical, hypocritical game I play.

A plank in my eye? Heck, I have an entire lumberyard in mine. As a leader; a friend; a dad; a husband a grandfather…I need to get rid of some wood.

Do not judge, or you too will be judged. For in the same way you judge others, you will be judged, and with the measure you use, it will be measured to you. Why do you look at the speck of sawdust in your brother's eye and pay no attention to the plank in your own eye? - Matthew 7:1-3 (NIV)

ACTION ITEM

Look in the mirror. Literally... look at yourself. Does this piece of wisdom apply to you? Have any "wood" that you should dispose of?

WEEK 24 - NOTES

WEEK 25
SPEAKING YOUR MIND...WITH FILTERS

I appreciate people who are direct. Their candor and frankness is refreshing, leaving very little room for doubt as to where they stand. Do you grow weary trying to figure out what some people *really* mean when they talk? There are times I go so far as to either interpret the exact opposite of what they say or dismiss them all together.

That being said, I do think we should apply filters to what we say. We need to consider the other person's perspective; his/her history; the feelings they may have; whether or not they are suffering from fatigue or grief or distractions.

So which is it? Direct and candid? Or filtered comments? No surprise...it's both/and, not either/or.

As a man named Paul once said, "Speak the truth... in love".

Instead, speaking the truth in love, we will grow to become in every respect the mature body of him who is the head, that is, Christ. – Ephesians 4:15 (NIV)

ACTION ITEM

Jot down your ideas on how and with whom you could be more diplomatic. Commit to giving a "kinder, gentler" approach without giving up your candor and truthfulness.

WEEK 25 - NOTES

WEEK 26
THE VIEW IS NOT ALWAYS CLEAR

If you zoom in and look closely perhaps you can see the base of the cloud-covered Sierra Blanca Mountain in New Mexico. From this view it is difficult to imagine a mountain being there at all. But whether you can see it or not, it's there.

The mountain offers the laughter of families…moms, dads, and kids…as they ski or snowboard. It offers the beautiful view of the surrounding peaks. It holds the mystery of nature including cold and wind and sun and warmth all within the same day. It seems to call you as only creation can.

My sons, son-in-law, and I answered the call this weekend and skied there together. And even though the mountain was shrouded in clouds when we left our cabin, it was there waiting for us when we arrived.

So it is with life. Sometimes it is shrouded in mystery and seems cold. Distant. Unfriendly. Perhaps unattainable. But we also know that life offers joy and beauty and laughter and friends and family.

Your life a bit cloudy right now? Stay with it. Don't give up. The clouds will lift and the sun (and joy) will return soon.

So do not throw away your confidence; it will be richly rewarded. – Hebrews 10:35 (NIV)

ACTION ITEM

This week list those things that are challenging you. Then revisit this page in a month (put a reminder on your calendar). See how many of those challenges have been met. You will be pleasantly surprised.

WEEK 26 – NOTES

WEEK 27
THE HARDER I WORK...

...the luckier I get. My father-in-law used to say that when people would say, "Linc, you sure are lucky!" He didn't disagree that he was, indeed, fortunate. But, he also stressed the fact that he made at least a part of that luck through his industriousness.

I co-facilitated a leadership institute a few years with Dr. Juan Munoz at Texas Tech. He did a fantastic job of teaching and inspiring the attendees. I learned a great deal from him. His subject matter centered primarily around "executive learning". He emphasized that much of that learning came from the pro-active, intentional, *hard work* that leaders must do to be...well, lucky.

In other words, planning (dreaming big dreams) AND execution (working hard) are needed to be both successful and significant. As someone once said, "Vision without execution is delusion".

The leadership lesson for this week? Work hard...get lucky.

All hard work brings a profit, but mere talk leads only to poverty. – Proverbs 14:23 (NIV)

ACTION ITEM

For this week honestly appraise how hard you are working. Not 24/7...you need to leave time for family, friends, & yourself. But, is there at least some small area of improvement you can identify?

WEEK 27 - NOTES

WEEK 28
ORDER VS. CHAOS

Simple question: Which is better... order or chaos? Simple answer: it depends. Obviously, in almost every case order beats the pants off of chaos. Some things are very easily ordered because we have nothing to do with them...the changing of the seasons; the 365-1/4 day trip of the earth around the sun; the regular beat of our hearts; the end of daylight followed by hours of darkness. All these are very orderly.

Other things are not so easily ordered, but we DO have the choice to bring order out of chaos, don't we? We *can* clean out the attic. We *can* make some sense of our schedule. We *can* create boundaries of what is acceptable and not acceptable behavior in our circle of influence. But all these "can-do's" come about because of conscious choices we make. They are not accidental; they are intentional.

Yet, there *are* some times that chaos is needed. The term disruptive innovation came to my attention today. To really change our world and the way we live, chaos may be needed during the midst of disruptive innovation. So, you see, chaos actually can lead to order. It's worth thinking about.

He has filled them with skill to do all kinds of work as engravers, designers, embroiderers in blue, purple and scarlet yarn and fine linen, and weavers—all of them skilled workers and designers. - Exodus 35:35 (NIV)

ACTION ITEM

Where can you bring order to your life this week as a leader? And how can you use creative, disruptive innovation to your advantage?

WEEK 28 – NOTES

WEEK 29
ARE WE TAKING THE TIME TO *REALLY* SEE?

As I watched an incredible sunrise this morning the question came to me, "am I taking the time to really see all that there is around me"? The quick and simple answer is "no". The more complex answer deals with schedules, pace, distractions, priorities, etc.

Here is what I took the time to see as the first glimpse of daylight appeared. A pallet of colors too diverse to describe. Could one have been umber? Trees stretching their limbs transforming the canopy into one of fingers reaching out to the sky. Water acting as a mirror to reflect the images cast into it. Ducks gliding across the surface of the lake. The grass wet from the morning dew.

As leaders, I wonder what we are missing in our people that we don't take the time to really see. I wonder…and today, I am going to look much more closely. There is wonder to grasp. There is potential to be filled. There is beauty to be admired. There is strength to be honored.

He makes me lie down in green pastures. He leads me beside waters of rest. He restores my soul. – Psalm 23:2-3a (NASB)

ACTION ITEM

Stop and think about what you may be missing in your relationships. Ask more questions out of genuine interest in people so you can get to know them better. By honoring them you will find the favor will be returned.

WEEK 29 – NOTES

WEEK 30
GRIEF

I WROTE THE FOLLOWING ON SEPTEMBER 4, 2014

I felt the need to say something special on September 1, 2014, the 2nd "anniversary" of Jayne Ann's last day on earth. But I struggled with what and how much to say. It's been years since that day in 2014, but here were my thoughts back then about Jammy (her grandmother nickname).

First, I still miss her. Not in a profound, painful way that I did during the months right after she died. But in a new and special way. I rarely miss her in a sad way. She is whole and complete. How can I be sad about that? Heck, maybe I'm just a little jealous that she beat me to the finish line!

Second, I have found that I have her "permission" to move on with my life. I know I've always had that, but now I am in an emotional position to act on it…to move on in a "fully alive" way, just as she would want.

Third, I no longer have to "man-up" and get on with life. Instead, I'm simply doing it. I'm pursuing joy and new relationships and this new era of life in a way that is refreshing. I'm older now, but there is still a little boy running around inside my head and heart. I find the pursuit to be effortless.

Thanks for letting me tell you some of my deepest thoughts.

Then he turned my sorrow into joy. He took away my clothes of mourning and clothed me with joy. – Psalm 30:11 (TLB)

ACTION ITEM

Take a few minutes this week to write down your deepest thoughts about something or someone you've lost. Wherever you are in your grief journey is OK. Just take it one day, one step at a time.

WEEK 30 - NOTES

WEEK 31
BE SPECIFIC

Sometimes a simple pat on the back or saying "good job" is all another needs to be encouraged.

You can go much deeper and get better responses, however, if you are specific. Such as:

"The timing of your comment regarding the Mitchell proposal was perfect. You have such a knack for saying the right thing at the right time."

"You handled the termination with just the right balance of courtesy and firmness. You treated him kindly while candidly pointing out the reasons for termination."

"Your friendship is invaluable to me. I could list reason after reason why you mean so much to me, but here are just two: your patience and your smile."

"Passing along the format you used in landing the Wilson account would be a great help to the firm. It was unique and effective."

It's the little words that mean a great deal to others. Choose and use them carefully and generously.

Pleasant words are like a honeycomb, sweetness to the soul and health to the body. – Proverbs 16:24 (NRSV)

ACTION ITEM

Ready. Set. Go! Find some specific praises you can give to your team this week. Be genuine and accurate and personal.

WEEK 31 - NOTES

WEEK 32
THINK ABOUT THIS: #1

For the next few weeks I'm going to share some quotations on leadership from other people. Some I knew of, others I'd never heard of before my research. But they all have ideas that are worth passing on to you. We can't grasp them all...so just take one each week and *apply it*. Just one...that's all.

Here's this week's.

You manage things; you lead people.
– Rear Admiral Grace Murray Hopper

Admiral Hopper (1906-1992) was a computer pioneer and naval officer. She earned a master's degree and a Ph.D. in mathematics from Yale. Hopper is best known for her trailblazing contributions to computer programming, software development and the design and implementation of programming languages. A maverick and an innovator, she enjoyed long and influential careers in the U.S. Navy and the computer industry. (Courtesy of Yale University)

Do nothing out of selfish ambition or vain conceit. Rather, in humility value others above yourselves. – Philippians 2:3 (NIV)

ACTION ITEM

Make 2 columns. In one list the things you manage. In the other, list all the people you lead. Now, focus on the people.

WEEK 32 - NOTES

WEEK 33
THINK ABOUT THIS: #2

A leader is a dealer in hope.
– Napoleon Bonaparte

Napoleon Bonaparte (1769-1821) was a French general and emperor of the French and was one of the most celebrated personages in the history of the West. He revolutionized military organization and training; sponsored the Napoleonic Code which became the prototype for later civil-law codes; reorganized education; and established the long-lived Concordat with the papacy. (Courtesy of Encyclopedia Britannica)

For I know the plans I have for you," declares the Lord, "plans to prosper you and not to harm you, plans to give you hope and a future. – Jeremiah 29:11 (NIV)

ACTION ITEM

Give people reasons to have hope.
Jot a few reasons down now.

WEEK 33 - NOTES

WEEK 34
THINK ABOUT THIS: #3

Pour it on 'em.
– Alex K. Miller

Circa 1957

Circa 1998

Note of personal privilege. My dad used to tell me this. It means to give it all I've got...to do my best. He wasn't just my dad. He was my confidant. Best man in my wedding. Hunting buddy. Business partner. Mentor. Model husband to Mom. The most influential leader in my life. Thanks, Dad. I'm still doing my best.

Whatever you do, work at it with all your heart...
– Colossians 3:23a (NIV)

ACTION ITEM

Are you working with all your heart (being wholehearted)? How can you "pour it on 'em this week?"

WEEK 34 - NOTES

WEEK 35
THINK ABOUT THIS: #4

I am reminded of how hollow the label of leadership sometimes is and how heroic followership can be.
– Warren Bennis

Warren Bennis (1925-2014) was an eminent scholar and author who advised presidents and business executives on his academic specialty, the essence of successful leadership. He was a distinguished professor of business administration at the University of Southern California. Professor Bennis wrote more than 30 books on leadership, a subject that grabbed his attention early in life when he led a platoon during World War II at the age of 19. (Courtesy of the New York Times)

We have enough material on leadership to last a lifetime. What we need is more on followership. Pay careful attention to this quote from ***Warren Bennis*** which supports that notion.

The fear of the Lord is the beginning of wisdom; all who follow his precepts have good understanding. – Psalm 111:10 (NIV)

ACTION ITEM

Jot down a few ideas on how you can be a "heroic follower."

WEEK 35 - NOTES

WEEK 36
THINK ABOUT THIS: #5

The key to successful leadership today is influence, not authority.
- Ken Blanchard

Few people have influenced the day-to-day management of people and companies more than Ken Blanchard. A prominent, sought-after author, speaker, and business consultant, Dr. Blanchard is respected for his lifetime of groundbreaking research and thought leadership. He has 60 books to his credit whose combined sales total more than 21 million copies. His groundbreaking works – including *Raving Fans, The Secret,* and *Leading at a Higher Level,* have been translated into more than 42 languages. (Courtesy of kenblanchard.com)

The good influence of godly citizens causes a city to prosper, but the moral decay of the wicked drives it downhill.
- Proverbs 11:11 (TLB)

ACTION ITEM

How can you optimize the use of your authority by increasing your influence on others?

WEEK 36 - NOTES

WEEK 37
THINK ABOUT THIS: #6

The growth and development of people is the highest calling of leadership.* – *Harvey Firestone

Henry Ford, Thomas Edison, & Harvey Firestone Ft. Myers, FL – 1929

Harvey S. Firestone (1868-1938) came up with ideas that forever changed how we get around on four wheels. His ideas were rooted in his work at his uncle's buggy company in Detroit. It wasn't long before he left his uncle's company and set off for Chicago. There Firestone founded his first tire business in 1897. He sold his stake two years later and put the proceeds toward launching The Firestone Tire & Rubber Co. in 1900 in Akron, Ohio. In its first year in business the company sold $110,000.00 in tires. Bridgestone eventually acquired the company and had revenues of $2.9 billion in 2020. (Courtesy of firestonecompleteautocare.com)

It took root and grew and became a low but spreading vine that turned toward the eagle and produced strong branches and luxuriant leaves. – Ezekiel 17:6 (TLB)

ACTION ITEM

Concentrate on only one person this week that you want to help grow and develop.

WEEK 37 – NOTES

WEEK 38
THINK ABOUT THIS: #7

Read good books because they will encourage as well as direct your feelings.* – *Thomas Jefferson

Thomas Jefferson (1743-1826) was the third president of the United States; vice president; secretary of state; diplomatic minister; and congressman. For his home state of Virginia he served as governor and member of the House of Delegates and the House of Burgesses. He was also a lawyer, architect, writer, farmer, scientist, and primary author of the declaration of independence. (Courtesy of Monticello.org)

What have you read lately?

***The one who gets wisdom loves life; the one who cherishes understanding will soon prosper. – Proverbs 19:8** (NIV)*

ACTION ITEM

Create a list of books to read in the next month. Can you read at least 2? 3? 4?

WEEK 38 – NOTES

WEEK 39
THINK ABOUT THIS: #8

When you can't make them see the light, make them feel the heat.
- Ronald Reagan

Ronald Reagan (1911-2004) was an American actor, governor of California, and because the 40th president of the United States, serving from 1981-1989. His term saw a restoration of prosperity at home with a goal of achieving "peace through strength" abroad. (Courtesy of the White House)

Sometimes, you have cowboy up.

Even in darkness light dawns for the upright, for those who are gracious and compassionate. - Psalm 112:4 (NIV)

ACTION ITEM

Is there someone that you need to turn the heat up on? Who? Why? How?

WEEK 39 - NOTES

WEEK 40
THINK ABOUT THIS: #9

Leadership is the art of getting someone to do something you want because he wants to do it.
– Dwight D. Eisenhower

Dwight D. Eisenhower (1809-1969) – was the supreme commander of the U.S. armed forces in Europe and later became the 34th President of the United States of America. He brought to the presidency his prestige as the commanding general of the victorious forces in Europe. He obtained a truce in Korea and worked incessantly during his two terms to ease the tensions of the Cold War. (Courtesy of the White House)

May he give you the desire of your heart and make all your plans succeed. – Psalm 20:4 (NIV)

ACTION ITEM

Write why people would want to do what you want them to do.

WEEK 40 - NOTES

WEEK 41
THINK ABOUT THIS: #10

You can have everything you want in life, if you will just help enough other people get what they want.
- Zig Ziglar

Zig Ziglar (1926-2012) is known as America's most influential and beloved encourager and believer that everyone could be, do, and have more. He founded the Zig Ziglar Corporation in 1977 and influenced an estimated quarter of a billion individuals through his 33 books, including the best seller, *See You at the Top*, which has sold almost two million copies. (Courtesy of ziglar.com)

This final quote in this series of ten is from one of the most inspirational speakers of our time.

Give, and it will be given to you. A good measure, pressed down, shaken together and running over, will be poured into your lap. For with the measure you use, it will be measured to you.
- Luke 6:38 (NIV)

ACTION ITEM

Think of who you can help get what they want (or need).

WEEK 41 - NOTES

WEEK 42
WHY NOT YOU?

Why not pursue that adventure?

Why not take that trip?

Why not ask her out?

Why not try something different...*really* different?

Why not take the risk?

Why not be in the top of the class?

Why not be the one people look to for solutions?

Why not change careers at age 60? or 30? Or whatever age you are.

No excuses. No alibis. No paralyzing fear. No "I could never do that".

Go for it. Somebody will. Why not YOU?

And who knows but that you have come to your royal position for such a time as this? – Esther 4:14b (NIV)

ACTION ITEM

Are you putting off your dream? Afraid of failing? What if you decided to "go for it"? As the next step, use your imagination and describe your dream on the opposite page.

WEEK 42 - NOTES

WEEK 43
MAKING IT IN THE MAJOR LEAGUE

Our son, Matt, pitched in the Detroit Tiger organization for six seasons, two of those as a reliever at the major league level for the Tigers. A shoulder injury that couldn't be corrected by multiple surgeries knocked him out of the game. But as his dad, boy was it fun to watch him play when it lasted!

From his experience I've concluded for any of us to "make it" wherever we are doing whatever we are doing, that three key ingredients are needed.

(1) Good genes. God-given ability. A natural talent. Call it what you want, but every one of us was born with some innate capability that had to come from a miraculous genetic code. *You have yours!* What is it?

(2) Luck. Divine plan. Good fortune. Again, you can assign your own word to it, but sooner or later we have good breaks that come our way. These are opportunities that were not your doing...they simply were blessings that you were given.

(3) Hard work. Listen, when you reach the level that Matt did *everyone* is talented and *everyone* has been "lucky". Therefore, without hard work you will get sent back down to the minor leagues real fast.

So which of these 3 do we have control over? Only working hard. Our natural talent is wasted unless we work diligently to use it. People ask what the secret to success is. Work your rear-end off. Show up. Sweat...not just a little, but a lot. Be able to look back and honestly tell yourself that you did the very best that you could with the talent you were given and the breaks that came your way.

Night and day we toiled and sweated to earn enough to live on so that our expenses would not be a burden to anyone there.
– 1 Thessalonians 2:9 (TLB)

ACTION ITEM

You know you have a gift of some kind that is special to you. What is it? Write about it here.

WEEK 43 - NOTES

WEEK 44
BE THERE

When our three children left for college I wrote each of them a letter giving some advice and expressing my love for them. I used a quote that I picked up somewhere along the way. That quote was "*Be there*".

One time my sister and her husband traveled from Texas to Atlanta where they watched one of their grandsons play in the World Wooden Bat Association National Championships. She said it was plenty hot and sticky. But he'll remember his grandparents were there.

In my previous career I traveled a good bit and had plenty of demands on my time at work, as you do. I would get our kids' events schedules (baseball, basketball, tennis, dance recitals, piano recitals, etc.) and put them on my calendar. I scheduled my work around their events and probably was able to make 90% of them. Why? I needed them to know that I would be there for them. Interesting that as adults they are my best friends today, isn't it?

When my late wife Jayne Ann was in her final days of her battle with lymphoma, she had a simple request: she asked for our presence...just to be around her. And, as she took her last breath we were there for her and with each other.

Please be there for whoever needs you. Cancel or postpone a meeting. Make a change in plans. The investment of your time will be returned to you many times over.

The above photo is from our granddaughter's high school graduation. We were there!

Let each of you look not only to his own interests, but also to the interests of others. – Philippians 2:4 (NRSV)

ACTION ITEM

Take a few minutes and put the important personal commitments you'd like or need to make on your calendar. Looking back someday you will be glad to be able to say "I was there."

WEEK 44 - NOTES

WEEK 45
PAY IT FORWARD

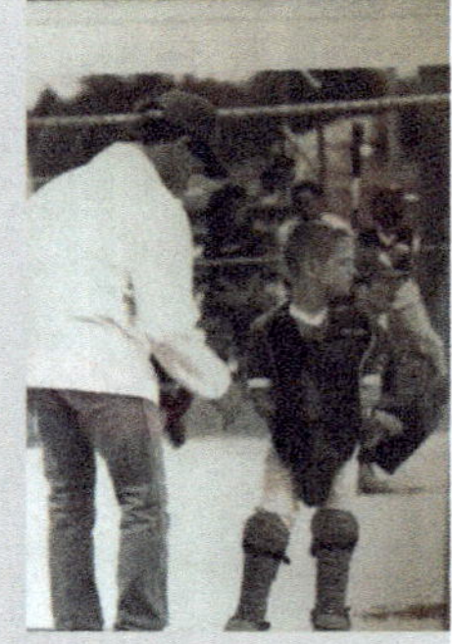
Me coaching my son, Tim – 1985

When I decided to create these weekly wisdom thoughts, the intention was just to take a brief part of your time for me to share a few thoughts on life and leadership. A couple hundred words. A few minutes of your time to read. Maybe another moment to *pay it forward* to others.

Today, I'm looking at the concept of a "moment" a bit differently. Really, all we have guaranteed is *this* day; *this* hour; *this* breath; *this moment.* And as I look back in time, especially with my children who now all have children of their own, I realize how important…no crucial…it is to pay forward what we have learned and experienced. Someone said we are only one generation from losing all we have worked and prayed for. Don't let that happen. Pay it forward.

Tim paying it forward to his son

The old saying, "yesterday's gone forever and tomorrow may never come" is 100% certain. Live in the moment. Enjoy the moment. Savor the moment. Treasure the moment. For *this* moment is the only one we really have.

You must teach them to your children and talk about them when you are at home or out for a walk; at bedtime and the first thing in the morning. – Deuteronomy 6:7 (TLB)

ACTION ITEM

Write down what and to whom you need to pay forward. Now put a deadline on getting it done.

WEEK 45 – NOTES

WEEK 46
MERCY

Restore.
Relieve.
Renew.
Recover.
Refresh.
Redeem.
Restart.

Aren't you glad we get chances to employ all of these liberating "re" words. Give yourself and others another chance today. The sun's coming up. It's a new day.

"The steadfast love of the Lord never ceases; his mercies never come to an end; they are new every morning; great is your faithfulness" – Lamentations 3:22-23 (ESV)

ACTION ITEM

Each day this week simply give thanks for the mercies you've been shown.

WEEK 46 – NOTES

WEEK 47
INTENTIONALITY

May 31, 1969. Landed. Honolulu. Joel, Jim, and me. Brand new, two-bedroom apartment on Liliuokalani Avenue about 3 blocks from Waikiki beach. Bought a dark green, 4-door, 1960 Ford Falcon (used more oil than gas). Neil Armstrong stepped onto the moon later that summer.

And a job for two months at Richmond Transfer & Storage. We moved military families in and out of homes. I've never been physically stronger in my life. The third month? Played and laughed and *lived… intentionally!*

The summer wasn't just about the beach or Diamond Head sunsets or coeds from some university in Austin or the paychecks from Richmond or the girls next door or the Primo beer or the moon landing or learning the difference between poi and pu pu (one is gross, the other delicious).

No, the entire experience was about *intentionality*. We decided to *do it…to go*.

We did it all *on purpose*. And until you and I *make up our minds to* _______________ (you fill in your blank and I'll fill in mine), it is highly unlikely that ____________________ will ever be realized.

Don't just dream it. Do it. And do it intentionally. 

"To everything there is a season, and a time to every purpose under the heaven." – Ecclesiastes 3:1 (NKJV)

ACTION ITEM

What will you decide to do on purpose this week? Be intentional. Stick with it. Do it.

WEEK 47 – NOTES

WEEK 48
THE CENTER OF HISTORY

As you read this I have no idea what happened on this date throughout history. But, I do believe that we are exactly in the center of eternal history. Note the word "eternal". I can't grasp what I'm about to suggest to you, but I believe it may have some merit anyway. Here goes...

If you think back in your mind as far back as possible...before the discovery of America, before biblical times, before dinosaurs, before...well, just keep going back and then add one more day back after that...then another. You never reach the end of past history. It's called infinity past, right?

Now reverse those thoughts and go forward into infinity. Past your children's and grandchildren's generation. Past putting humans on other planets. Now add another day or week. The future just keeps going and going.

If you *could* imagine the two points in time that represent the "beginning" and "end" of time and divide that timeline in half, where would the mid-point be?

TODAY, that's where.

So, today (and tomorrow and the next day) couldn't it be possible that we are living in the center of eternal history? Therefore, today must be a *really important day*. So let's live like it. Let's take advantage of the most precious gift any of us have. The gift of living life *today*.

He has made everything beautiful in its time. He has also set eternity in the human heart; yet no one can fathom what God has done from beginning to end. – Ecclesiastes 3:11 (NIV)

ACTION ITEM

Changing your perspective from a brief timeline to one that is much longer. Jot down your thoughts about your roles in life today. You are making an impact on others. It will last a long time.

WEEK 48 – NOTES

WEEK 49
LAUGHTER

Laughter. The kind that makes your stomach hurt.

The kind that makes you cover your mouth with your hand and close your eyes as they begin to leak happy tears.

The kind that when you look at your laughing partner you start laughing all over again.

The kind that you try to suppress in a movie or a restaurant or church, but whatever you're laughing about is just too funny to be suppressed.

The kind that makes milk shoot out of your nose.

The Jerry Seinfeld-George Costanza-Cosmo Kramer-Elaine Benes kind of one-liners. Matt and his brother, Tim, have every line of Seinfeld memorized…as they do every line of the movie *Airplane*. When these two get going, get out the Kleenex because you'll be laughing funny tears.

The kind that when you think about it a week or month or years later you chuckle and smile.

In fact, I'm smiling right now…

We were filled with laughter, and we sang for joy.
– Psalm 126:2a (NLT)

ACTION ITEM

Look for the fun and funny parts of life this week (and next).
Don't let your bones dry up.
Find something to laugh about with someone.

WEEK 49 - NOTES

WEEK 50
WHERE WERE YOU?

Where were you at his birthday party?

Where were you when the space shuttle went down?

Where were you when Kennedy was shot?

Where were you when Kirk Gibson hit his dramatic homerun for the Dodgers?

Where were you when Neil Armstrong took the first step on the moon?

Where were you on 9-11?

Where were you when your grade-schooler won the spelling bee?

Where were you at supper last night as it grew cold on the table at home?

Where were you when she hit the winning free-throw?

Where were you when she missed what could have been the winning free-throw?

Where were you when they really needed you?

This is not the time to pull away and neglect meeting together, as some have formed the habit of doing. In fact, we should come together even more frequently, eager to encourage and urge each other onward as we anticipate that day dawning.
– Hebrews 10:25 (TPT)

ACTION ITEM

It's never too late. So answer the following question by filling in the blank.

***Where* will I be when___________________________________?**

WEEK 50 – NOTES

WEEK 51
GRATITUDE

As I write this we are entering the third year of the CoVid 19 pandemic. Another surge has hit the intensive care units all across America.

Not too long ago 13 of our servicemen were killed at the Kabul airport by suicide bombers. Others were wounded. Many Afghan citizens died or were hurt at the hands of these terrorists.

A close friend of our daughter and son-in-law was diagnosed with 4th stage colon cancer. He has a wife and two young children

But, when I examine my life I almost feel guilty for how fortunate I am. I have my health, my wonderful wife, my terrific children and their spouses, incredibly talented and good-looking grandchildren, a comfortable house to live in, friends who are priceless, a faith that is strong.

Almost guilty? Yes, almost. Because instead I've chosen gratitude. I'm thankful that I have all I have, including many personal trials and challenges. They make me stronger. They keep me humble. They change my myopic perspective. I may not like the trials, but I do my very best to find the benefit they will bring. I am grateful, indeed.

Reading suggestion: Pick up the book *One Thousand Gifts* by Ann Voskamp. You will be grateful that you did.

"... we rejoice in our sufferings, knowing that suffering produces endurance, and endurance produces character, and character produces hope..." – Romans 5:3-4 (ESV)

ACTION ITEM

Start listing all the gifts of this life and the one to come you are grateful for. Include the good and the not-so-good. If you're serious about it, the list will go on and on and on.

WEEK 51 - NOTES

WEEK 52
FAITH

A few years ago I saw the movie "Heaven is for Real". Based on the book by the same name, the real-life story is about a little boy who, during a life-threatening surgery, has a near-death out-of-body experience in which he gets to visit heaven. The people he saw and the reports that he gives to his parents upon returning are amazing.

Do you believe in heaven? Is it for real?

What I *can* tell you is that there is heaven and hell here on earth. I've seen and experienced heights of joy that are unimaginable, asking "why me?" because I feel so fortunate. Yet, I've also experienced dark, painful episodes that simply make me ask "why does it have to be this way at all?" I haven't found an answer to either question (other than biased theological positions that people try to convince me of).

Here is what I *believe* based on *faith*. I believe that God is real. I believe that God is love. I believe he has prepared a place for us that is unimaginably perfect. And I believe that his ways and thoughts are so far above mine that my mind and heart might just explode if I knew the answers to these unanswerable questions.

For now, that is. I also believe that when I do die and leave this earth…this body…that all the answers to my questions will be perfect ones. And that the joys of "heaven on earth" will be infinitely surpassed by those we will know when we cross over.

Leadership point: you may not be able to answer all the questions that people ask you. It's ok. You don't have to know all the answers. Just hang on to your faith.

"No eye has seen, no ear has heard, and no mind has imagined what God has prepared for those who love him."
– 1 Corinthians 2:9 (NLT)

ACTION ITEM

When all else is lost you can still cling to your faith. Reflect on that and jot down your thoughts.

WEEK 52 - NOTES

APPENDICES AND WORKSHEETS

On the following pages you will find a variety of worksheets that will help reinforce your learning of some of the leadership ideas you've read about. For further explanation contact:

David A. Miller
david@davidmiller.pro

10 - 7 - 5

You can trace in part who you've become in life to three types of external factors: defining moments; critical choices; and pivotal people. First, let's understand those terms.

Ten Defining Moments: In your life there have been moments, both positive and negative, that have defined and redefined who you have become. Those events entered your consciousness with such power that they changed the very core of who you are. You had no control over these events and they didn't happen because of something you did or didn't do. A part of you was changed by these events and caused you to define yourself, to some degree, by having had these experiences. Examples: My mom died on the operating table. My best friend moved to a distant city. I was born and raised in Germany. My uncle left me a million dollars.

Seven Critical Choices: There are a surprisingly small number of choices that rise to the level of being life-changing. Critical choices are those that have changed your life, positively or negatively, and are major factors in determining who and what you will become. They are choices you made that have affected your life up to today and have set you on a path. Examples: Who you chose to marry. Where you went to college. What career you are pursuing. How you invest the million dollars from your uncle.

Five Pivotal People: These are the people who have left indelible impressions on your concept of self and therefore, the life you live. They may be family members, friends or co-workers, and their influences can be either positive or negative. They are people who can determine whether you live consistently with your authentic self or instead live a counterfeit life controlled by a fictional self that has crowded out who you really are.

Use the following page to define your external factors. It helps to do this in a small group of 3-4 people and discuss your responses. You'll be surprised at how much you have in common while at the same time having unique experiences.

Ten Defining Moments

1. ______________________________
2. ______________________________
3. ______________________________
4. ______________________________
5. ______________________________
6. ______________________________
7. ______________________________
8. ______________________________
9. ______________________________
10. ______________________________

Seven Critical Choices

1. ______________________________
2. ______________________________
3. ______________________________
4. ______________________________
5. ______________________________
6. ______________________________
7. ______________________________

Five Pivotal People

1. ______________________________
2. ______________________________
3. ______________________________
4. ______________________________
5. ______________________________

CLOSING THE ACCOUNTABILITY GAP

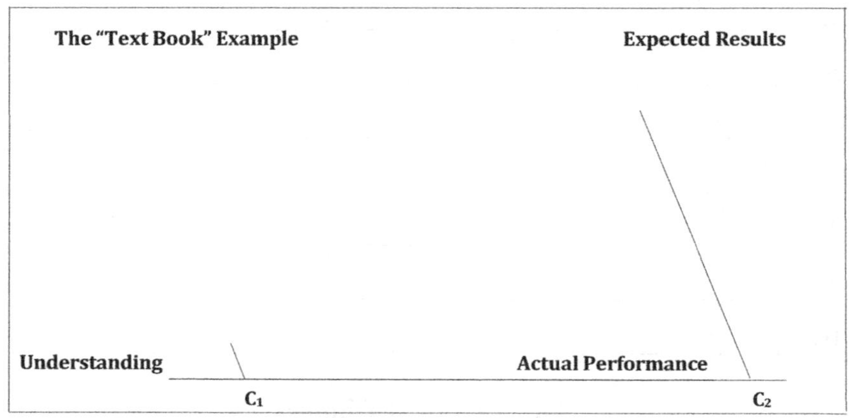

C1 = Correction (think course correction as you drive a car)
C2 = Crisis (think misery when a relationship is in turmoil)

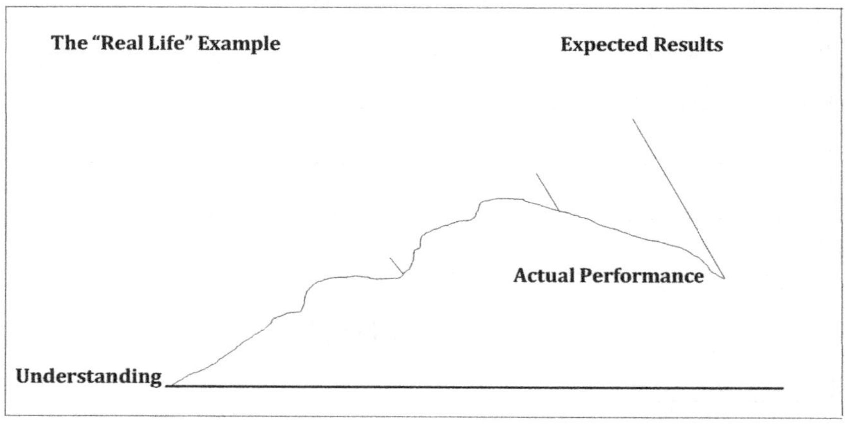

ACCOUNTABILITY - CLOSING THE GAP BETWEEN EXPECTATIONS AND PERFORMANCE

The Gap

What was expected (agreed upon)? ____________________

What actually happened? ____________________________

Diagnosis

Single occurrence ____________________________________

Trending ____

Trust ____

Safety Zone

Flight____

Fight ____

Preparation

Gather facts and stick with them ____________________

Ask for the other person's facts _____________________

Define in writing your desired outcome _______________

Anticipate the reaction from the other person ___________

Be prepared to state how you feel ____________________

Ask the other person how they feel ___________________

Determine the real reason for the gap

Inadequate commitment ______________________________

Negative peer pressure_______________________________

System problems ___________________________________

Lack of capability __________________________________

Team dysfunctional _________________________________

More resources needed ______________________________

Follow-up

State your conclusion________________________________

Reach revised, agreed upon expectations ______________

Make clear the benefits/consequences ________________

Schedule the next meeting___________________________

State what is different because of this meeting____________

CONFRONTATION MINUS FEAR OF CONFLICT EQUALS RESOLUTION

Holding conversations that make a difference requires:

1. Perspective
   a. Problems lead to profit______________________
   b. Don't avoid negatives – seek them out __________
   c. Consider problems as opportunities ____________

2. Resolve
   a. Confront reality ___________________________
   b. Keep the faith _____________________________
   c. Focus on desired outcome____________________

3. Assess
   a. Gather information _________________________
   b. Evaluate _________________________________
   c. Reconvene________________________________

4. Separation
   a. Address the problem, not the person ___________
   b. Consider all possible options _______________
   c. Deliver good news along with the bad __________

5. Ownership
   a. The Coachable ____________________________
   b. The Blamer _______________________________
   c. The Toxic ________________________________

6. Strategies
   a. The Coachable ____________________________
   b. The Blamer _______________________________
   c. The Toxic ________________________________

CONFRONTATION - FEAR OF CONFLICT = RESOLUTION

Understanding that holding conversations which make a difference requires perspective, resolve, assessment, separation, ownership, and strategy, create the best steps for your next critical conversation.

1. What is your perspective? What do you believe the other party's perspective is? Which is most realistic?
   Yours ____
   Theirs____
   Most realistic____________________________________

2. Are you resolved to work things out for both parties?
   Are you clear on the *facts?* ____________________________
   What is the desired outcome? ___________________________
   Is there possible win/win? _____________________________

3. Is your assessment complete?
   What additional info is needed? ________________________
   Is your evaluation finished? ___________________________
   When is the follow-up? ______________________________

4. Have you created emotional separation from the issue and the person?
   Are you addressing the problem, not the person? ___________
   Have you explored all optional outcomes? ________________
   Will you deliver good news with the bad? _________________

5. Is the other party taking appropriate ownership of the issue?
   Do you believe the other party is coachable? Yes_______ No ________
   Why do you think so? ________________________________
   Does the other party almost always place blame elsewhere? Yes__ No _
   Why do you think so? ________________________________
   Is the other party being toxic? Yes____________No ____________
   Why do you think so? ________________________________

6. Do you have clear strategic options going into the conversation?
   Your strategy for the coachable in this case is________________
   Your strategy for the blamer in this case is _________________
   Your strategy for the toxic in this case is___________________

DELEGATION WORKSHEET

What can (or should) I delegate?

What do I want to accomplish when I delegate it?

To **whom** shall I delegate it?

Why is this task important?

What resources will I provide when I delegate it?

Have I clarified the authority to whom I'm delegating?

How will I measure and communicate success?

When will I follow up?

Write down the benefits to you, the organization, and the person to whom you are delegating

ELEMENTS OF A GOOD MEETING

Steps	Element	Responsible Party	Done
1	Determine who should attend (need to know basis)		
2	Have the right number in attendance (stay small)		
3	Shared agenda (get input from others for agenda; set expectations)		
4	Use the most effective invitation method (email, phone, etc.)		
5	Clarify if attendance is mandatory or optional (people are busy)		
6	Ask for RSVP's to confirm attendees (who's coming or not)		
7	Specific agenda items (state anticipated outcomes; eliminate generalities)		
8	Adequate preparation (data, supporting documents, presentation material)		
9	Confirm logistical arrangements (room, A-V, dial-in & access code, etc.)		
10	Start on time (whether everyone is present or not)		
11	Agreement for everyone to be engaged (no sleepers)		
12	Create/maintain a safe meeting environment (build trust)		
13	Have conversational dialogue (involve others; don't let anyone dominate)		
14	Keep on track (stay focused - don't wander)		
15	Build consensus (not necessarily unanimity; different ideas are welcome)		
16	Reach conclusions/make decisions (whenever possible)		
17	Verbally employ at least one company Value (keep values visible)		
18	Depart with action items (accountability counts... what, when, who)		
19	End on time (respect everyone's time)		
20	Leave the space nicer than you found it (golden rule)		

THE FOUR CORNERSTONES

Trust requires:

1. Wholeheartedness
2. Competence
3. Alignment
4. Production

Understanding includes:

1. Discovering
2. Clarifying
3. Questioning
4. Confirming

Freedom allows:

1. Innovation/Failure
2. Challenge
3. Ownership
4. Fun

Unity promotes:

1. Encouragement
2. Grace
3. Compassion
4. Strength

And, the capstone

Joy results in:

1. Calm
2. Contentment
3. Confidence
4. Completion

THE FOUR CORNERSTONES

Trust requires:

1. Wholeheartedness (Integrity)
2. Competence
3. Alignment
4. Production

Understanding includes:

1. Discovering
2. Clarify (Parrot back)
3. Questioning
4. Confirming (in writing)

Freedom allows:

1. Innovative and Fail
2. Challenge each other
3. Ownership
4. Fun

Unity promotes:

1. Encouragement (of the whole heart)
2. Grace
3. Compassion
4. Strength

And, the capstone

JOY results in:

1. Calm
2. Contentment
3. Confidence
4. Completion

THE FOUR CORNERSTONES AND THE EVALUATION PROCESS

Stop...Look...Listen. Prior to an annual evaluation, informal review, necessary critique, crucial conversation, performance change agreement, final warning, and/or termination, consider these questions. NOTE: Always confer with your HR personnel regarding use of these questions.

1. Has this person been ***trust***worthy and ***trust***ing in others regarding:
   a. Being wholehearted in their efforts? And, have I?
   b. Has proven to be competent in meeting the requirements of their assignments? And, have I?
   c. Aligning with our strategies and goals as well as our vision, mission, and values? And, am I?
   d. Producing desired and expected results? And, am I?
2. Do we have a clear ***understanding*** of what expectations are?
   a. Has all necessary information been properly provided? And, have I made sure it has?
   b. Did this person clarify my instructions? And, did I?
   c. Did they ask questions about the expectation? And, did I give them adequate opportunity?
   d. Did we mutually confirm performance expectations? Was I responsible for this?
3. Does this person contribute to the atmosphere of ***freedom*** within the organization?
   a. Do they demonstrate innovative thinking and risk taking? Do I encourage new ideas/methods?
   b. Do they challenge ideas, assumptions, and "old-way" thinking? Do I allow them to do so?
   c. Do they share in holding each themselves accountable? Do I assure such ownership?
   d. Do they enjoy work and have fun? Do I?
4. Has this employee added to the ***unity*** of the organization?
   a. Do they encourage others, including fellow employees? How am I doing in this area?
   b. Do they have compassion for others? Am I setting an example of compassion?
   c. Do they practice giving and receiving grace? Do I??
   d. Do they add strength to the organization? What have I done to strengthen the team?

THE FOUR CORNERSTONES AND THE HIRING PROCESS

The application of the Four Cornerstones during the hiring process is essential in maintaining the excellence of the team. NOTE: Always confer with your HR personnel regarding use of these questions.

1. Is there a strong sense of ***trust*** related to:
   a. The candidate's wholeheartedness (will they give it their *all*)?
   b. The candidate's competence in meeting the requirements of the job description?
   c. The candidate's alignment with our vision, mission, and values?
   d. The candidate's track record of delivering expected production?

2. Has the opportunity been given to all parties to have a clear ***understanding*** through:
   a. Discuss job requirements (hours, travel, speaking, organizational structure, etc.)?
   b. Clarify the requirements of the position and the person filling it?
   c. Ask questions pertinent to the position and organization?
   d. Confirm performance expectations?

3. Will this person contribute to the atmosphere of ***freedom*** within the organization that includes:
   a. Innovative thinking; creating new ideas? Understanding errors are going to happen?
   b. Challenging ideas and assumptions and "old-way" thinking?
   c. Holding each other accountable for our commitments?
   d. Letting go and having fun?

4. Does the candidate add to the ***unity*** of the organization by:
   a. Encouraging others, including fellow employees?
   b. Having compassion for others?
   c. Giving and receiving grace?
   d. Providing additional strength to the organization?

THAT'S A *GOOD* IDEA!

I need to take action on this good idea:

I should pass this idea along to:

I will file this idea away for use in the future:

GRATITUDE!

I like my job because ____________________

I like my job because ____________________

I like my job because ____________________

I like my job because ____________________

I like my job because ____________________

I like my job because ____________________

I like my job because ____________________

I like my job because ____________________

I like my job because ____________________

I like my job because ____________________

I like my job because ____________________

I like my job because ____________________

I like my job because ____________________

I like my job because ____________________

I like my job because ____________________

I like my job because ____________________

Today I'm going to tell ____________ what I like about my job.
(Name of Person)

Tonight before I go to sleep I'm going to remember

____________________ about my job.
(something good)

When I wake up in the morning I will remember

____________________ about my job.
(something good)

ORGANIZATIONAL STRATEGIC PLANNING AND THE FOUR CORNERSTONES

1. Trust
    a. Does our plan stretch us, requiring us to give our integrity (our whole selves) while simultaneously keeping our lives in balance between family, career, community, friends?
    b. Does our plan go beyond our competence; i.e., is it realistic or a pipe dream?
    c. Is our plan aligned with our values; our families' needs; the organization's vision and mission?
    d. Will our plan produce results that not only reach certain goals, but also create a positive difference in the lives of others?

2. Understanding
    a. Does our plan create the desire for more learning; more discovery?
    b. Have we clarified our plan by writing it in different ways; using different words and priorities?
    c. Has our plan been reviewed by the appropriate people who will ask penetrating questions?
    d. Have we confirmed that the plan is solid – one that can make a real difference in our organization's future?

3. Freedom
    a. Is our plan innovative and full of fresh, perhaps even radical, ideas? Are we taking smart chances leaving room for adjustment when errors or the unexpected occur?
    b. Have we given others (and ourselves) permission to challenge us as we carry out the plan?
    c. Who has the authority and responsibility to hold us accountable to our plan?
    d. Will we have fun executing the plan?

4. Unity
    a. Where or to whom do we go for encouragement when the going gets tough?
    b. Will we give ourselves grace when we fall short?
    c. Does our plan show compassion for others, including people who are different from us?
    d. How does our plan result in a strengthened life, family, organization, career, community?

And, for the capstone…

- Joy
    - o Does our plan bring a measure of calm to our life and those around us?
    - o Will we find contentment when our plan is executed in reality?
    - o How does our plan increase our level of confidence in ourselves and others surrounding us?
    - o Does our plan result in a sense of completion…of accomplishment…of victory?

PERSONAL STRATEGIC PLANNING AND THE FOUR CORNERSTONES

Trust

- Does my plan stretch me, requiring me to give my integrity (my whole self) while simultaneously keeping my life in balance between family, career, community, friends?
- Does my plan go beyond my capability/capacity; i.e., is it realistic or a pipe dream?
- Is my plan aligned with my values; my families' needs; my organization's vision and mission?
- Will my plan produce results that not only reach certain goals, but also create a positive difference in the lives of others?

Understanding

- Does my plan create the desire for more learning; more discovery?
- Have I clarified my plan by writing it in different ways; using different words and priorities?
- Has my plan been reviewed by at least one other person that will ask penetrating questions?
- Have I confirmed that the plan is solid – one that can make a real difference in my life?

Freedom

- Is my plan innovative and full of fresh, perhaps even radical, ideas? Am I giving myself freedom to make mistakes and move on?
- Have I given others (and myself) permission to challenge me as I carry out the plan?
- Who have I given the authority and responsibility to hold me accountable to my plan?
- Will I have fun living out my life plan?

Unity

- Where or to whom do I go for encouragement when the going gets tough?
- Will I give myself grace when I fall short?
- Does my plan show compassion for others, including people who are different from me?
- How does my plan result in a strengthened life, family, organization, career, community?

And, for the capstone…Joy

- Does my plan bring peace to my life and those around me?
- Will I find contentment when my plan is executed in reality?
- How does my plan increase my level of confidence in myself and others surrounding me?
- Does my plan result in a sense of completion…of accomplishment…of a victorious life?

PERSONAL LEADERSHIP SWOT ANALYSIS

Evaluate yourself as a leader as you see yourself *today* … not how others see you or how you want to be seen, but how you really think you are today. Use the SWOT spaces below to establish a benchmark that you can use later to measure your progress.

Strengths (positive *internal* characteristics of mine that I should take advantage of)

____

____

____

Weaknesses (*internal* challenges that are negative traits of mine and need to be eliminated or reduced)

____

____

____

Opportunities (*external* possibilities that I should consider that would enhance my leadership)

____

____

____

Threats (things that are *external* which I have no control over, but could be a problem for me)

____

____

____

PURPOSE, VISION, MISSION, AND VALUES WORKSHEET

To get you started on the challenging task of identifying your vision, mission, and values, answer the following questions as honestly and completely as you can. Use just a few words, but make them powerful, impactful, and meaningful. This is *your* worksheet and this process is personal so dig deep to find *your* answers.

What do I want to be remembered for? What do I said about me at my funeral? What will be etched on my tombstone?

____

____

Who are the most important people in my life? Who do I love and want to be loved by? Who *really* matters most to me?

____

____

What do I love doing? What do I have a passion for? What am I pretty darn good at doing? What makes me feel "alive"?

____

____

In your mind, what is the difference between success and significance? Which would you choose if you could only have one?

____

____

If you could choose any career or vocation in the world, what would it be? Don't worry about money.

___

___

What principles or values are most important to you? What issues would you "fall on the sword" for?

___

___

What is one thing you don't like about yourself? What would you like to change? List ONLY one.

___

___

Who do you look up to? Who do you consider to be a hero in your life? Name all you can.

___

___

Think 20 years into the future. You've achieved all you wanted to achieve. What are those accomplishments?

___

___

WRITING PURPOSE, VISION, MISSION, AND VALUES STATEMENTS

Both as individuals and as organizations we need to look into our future and begin working on our thoughts which become our actions which become our habits which become our character which become our destiny. We begin with the end in mind by establishing our purpose, mission, vision, and values statements.

Purpose Statement

The purpose statement answers the question "*why* are we doing what we are doing?" It is our noble purpose; should not change; is far-reaching; unites our people; and defines the legacy we want to be remembered for.

____

____

Mission Statement

The mission statement answers the question "*what* are we doing?" It confirms that we are working for our purpose and toward our vision. It is strong, but flexible and should be reviewed from time to time; it is what we do; and it is achievable.

____

____

Vision Statement

The vision statement describes "what our purpose *looks like* when it is achieved". It is a picture in our minds of completion. In our imaginations it is ideal. We feel a great sense of unity, comradery, and satisfaction when we capture the vision.

____

____

Values Statement

The values statement expresses "how we *behave* as we go about our lives". It reflects our attitude and our character and sets standards by which we expect to be held accountable. These are non-negotiable principles.

____

____

Strategies and Goals

These strategies are the only major topics to be focused on in the coming year. They are critical success factors that cannot be ignored.

Strategy 1 ______________________________

Goal 1.1 ______________________________

Goal 1.2 ______________________________

Goal 1.3 ______________________________

Strategy 2 ______________________________

Goal 2.1 ______________________________

Goal 2.2 ______________________________

Goal 2.3 ______________________________

Strategy 3 ______________________________

Goal 3.1 ______________________________

Goal 3.2 ______________________________

Goal 3.3 ______________________________

NOTE: Each Goal and subsequent action item must be SMART: Specific – Measurable – Aligned – Realistic – Timely

QUESTIONS - TOUGH QUESTIONS

What are you afraid of and why?

What are you attached to and why?

What are you building toward and what progress are you making?

What's in your way and what are you going to do to remove it?

What if there were no limits to your current position? What would happen?

What has you stumped and what are you doing to solve it?

What is your biggest, wildest dream in life?

What do you want to be able to say about yourself this time next year?

What consumes your time that distracts you from attaining your goals?

THE FIRST PERSON

The first person I would want to know of a promotion at work is ______________________________

The first person I would want to take an around the world vacation with is ______________________

The first person I call to let them know that I'm home safely is ______________________________

The first person I think of as a great boss is ______________

The first person I need to forgive is ____________________

The first person I would want to talk to in heaven is _______

The first person I would want to be contacted if I was seriously injured is____________________________

The first person I need to thank is ____________________

The first person I would want to help me make a major decision is ______________________________

The first person I would be willing to share my deepest secret is ______________________________

And now. Who is the first person that you need to contact and (a) say you love them; (b) thank them; (c) forgive them?

______________ ______________ ______________

And when, where, how are you going to contact that person (those persons)?

When?__________ Where?__________ How? __________

YOUR LEGACY OF LEADERSHIP

Whether you think you are or not and whether you want to or not, you are leaving a legacy of leadership. Regardless of your position(s) in life (spouse, parent, friend, team member, etc.), you have no choice but to leave a legacy. Because, you see, your legacy is a gift to others...it is your story that they will continue to tell even after you can no longer tell it yourself.

It is proven that the more people know you (and your story) the more likely they are to follow your leadership and therefore reach the mutual goals of the leader and the follower. Therefore, this exercise is about helping you tell your story.

Complete the following using seven (7) words or LESS for each response.

My greatest strength is ______________________________

My greatest weakness is ______________________________

My fondest aspiration (dream) is ______________________

One of my life's biggest disappointments wa ____________

I still have some confusion about _____________________

One of my vulnerable spots is _________________________

Who has had the most influence on you in your professional life? ________

What ticks you off? __________________________________

Think of a failure you've had and write down how you recovered from it or tell what you learned from it.

____

Give one reason why you want to have the job you have now.

____

YOUR LEGACY OF LEADERSHIP - CONTINUED

We all talk about other people. What will people say about you when they speak of your legacy? What stories will other people tell about you? What will others learn from those stories? What is the legacy that you *want* to pass along? What am I learning from others as I teach?

ACKNOWLEDGEMENTS

Acknowledging all the people who poured into my life and, therefore, this book and its ideas reminds me of people accepting Emmy's or Oscar's who say "there are so many people to thank". Well, I have neither the talent nor the desire to receive such recognition, yet I do feel somewhat overwhelmed by the debt of gratitude I owe to so many. But, as I say in chapter nine, I just need to begin.

So, I will begin with people who have shepherded me in my career. Lewie Bates, Nagle Bridwell, Randal Caldwell, Charlie Cricks, and Jay Eagan to name a few. Their collective wisdom would fill many books. Thank you for allowing me to lean on you as a young man.

I'm grateful for those faithful team mates at The MED Group such as Monica Young, David Low, Kevin Davenport, Teresa Sparkman, and Jeff Woodham. There are many others, of course, but these folks have been kind to keep in touch through the years after our work days together were completed. They taught me the value of how a leader should also be a good follower and I was honored to have learned from them.

James Cutrera, Michelle Cook, Mariano Villalobos, Jim Shearer, Todd Wyrick, and Mark Persall are saints in my eyes for the work they did at our team and leadership development retreat known as Spirit Ranch. Their servant's hearts remain a model for me today and many of their thoughts are woven into the words of this book.

Where would I be today without "The Twelve" from our high school days? Graduating in 1967 did not deter us from staying close. Two are gone from this earth now and one has "opted out". But, nine of us are still going strong. Thank you Steve and Stan Hurt, Steve Moore, Dale and Gale Lewis, Randy Andrews, Jim O'Jibway, and John Owens. No one could ask for better friends than you.

Bobby Steiner, director of golf at Horseshoe Bay (and my personal trainer) not only encouraged me, but directed me to resources that I otherwise would have struggled finding. He is a positive accountability partner, for sure.

Pat Schoch served as my editor and helped introduce me to the world of writing. I'm grateful for this neighbor who is also a heck of a golfer.

Amy Vaughn of Soundview Design simply could not have been more accommodating, professional, prompt, and courteous. I have her to thank for the layout of the book and the cover design.

And, the proverbial "last, but not least" is my wife Katherine. Her patience and encouragement were such a boost to me throughout the process. What a partner you are, Kid!

ENDNOTES

1 Jim Collins, Brene Brown, Stephen Covey, Patrick Lencioni, Ken Blanchard, Peter Drucker, Tom Peters, Malcolm Gladwell, Simon Sinek, John Maxwell, Bob Biehl, Henry Cloud, John Townsend

2 https://www.worldatlas.com/articles/man-in-the-arena.html

3 https://lauriebethjones.com/

4 John 14:6

5 Isaiah 61:1

6 https://www.ransomedheart.com/daily-reading/sacred-romance

7 https://www.ransomedheart.com/

8 Also attributed to Howard Thurman https://www.azquotes.com/author/14651-Howard_Thurman

9 https://thestellarfamily.com/the-stellar-family/leadership-2/steve-hurt.html

10 Randy Andrews is the founder and president of GRACO http://www.gracorealestate.com/about-us

11 https://www.christianity.com/

12 Earnings Before Interest Taxes Depreciation Amortization; Cost of Goods Sold; Long Term Value

13 https://www.lexico.com/en/definition/empower

14 https://www.speedoftrust.com/

15 https://www.investopedia.com/articles/investing/072315/4-things-you-didnt-know-about-southwest-airlines.asp

16 https://hbr.org/1957/09/listening-to-people

17 https://www.post-it.com/3M/en_US/post-it/contact-us/about-us/

18 https://www.smithsonianmag.com/innovation/7-epic-fails-brought-to-you-by-the-genius-mind-of-thomas-edison-180947786/

19 Ecclesiastes 2:24

20 https://www.etymonline.com/word/courage

21 Philippians 4:11-12

22 https://www.tecovas.com/

23 https://quotationcelebration.wordpress.com/2018/01/29/though-you-can-easily-count-the-seeds-in-an-apple-its-impossible-to-count-the-apples-in-a-seed/

24 https://marthabeck.com/2012/02/making-time-for-nothing/

ABOUT THE AUTHOR

Raised on the South Plains of West Texas, David Miller graduated from Texas Tech University with a degree in Administrative Management. David was married to Jayne Ann Williston of Austin for 40+ years before losing her to cancer. He is now married to the former Katherine McKelvy and resides in Horseshoe Bay, Texas. Together they have four children... Tim, Matt, Beth, and Summer…and nine grandchildren.

The author and his wife, Katherine

David invested 34 years of his career in the medical equipment industry, 14 of those as the owner and operator of a small retail company with three Texas locations. Then, for the next 20 years he was the CEO of The MED Group, a national business services organization that, with his outstanding team, grew from 27 locations to over 800.

In 2005, David founded Spirit Ranch, a leadership and team development retreat center in Lubbock, Texas. His vision was to bring others closer to their Creator. The mission was to build believers, leaders, and teams. The Spirit Ranch team served over 30,000 guests and clients in pursuit of that vision and mission. The transformation in people's lives and, therefore, their organizations and families, has been amazing.

In addition to serving as mayor of Lubbock, Texas, David was a member of the boards of directors for University Medical Center, United Way, Lubbock Chamber of Commerce, Lubbock National Bank, Texas Tech Alumni Association, and volunteered for many other local, state, and national organizations. His desire is to pay forward the time-tested tenants of leadership through personal coaching, group facilitation and public speaking.

For more information visit www.cornerstoneexecutives.com.